Queer Magic Photo Zine—Albany   October 2021

QUEER MAGIC ALBANY
PHOTO ZINE

©LOUD & QUEER and Aries I Am Production   Angel Angeles & Marisa Wohlschlaeger

Creator, Photographer, & Model	Instagram
Angel Angeles	areisiam & ariesiamproduction
Marisa Wohlschlaeger	marisatherainbow & loudandqueerzine

Brands	
The Phluid Project	thephluidproject
Gemder Fluid Designs	gemder.fluid.designs
Spiritually Stoned Co	spiritually_stonedco
	moniautumn

Photo Location—Albany Bulb, Albany CA

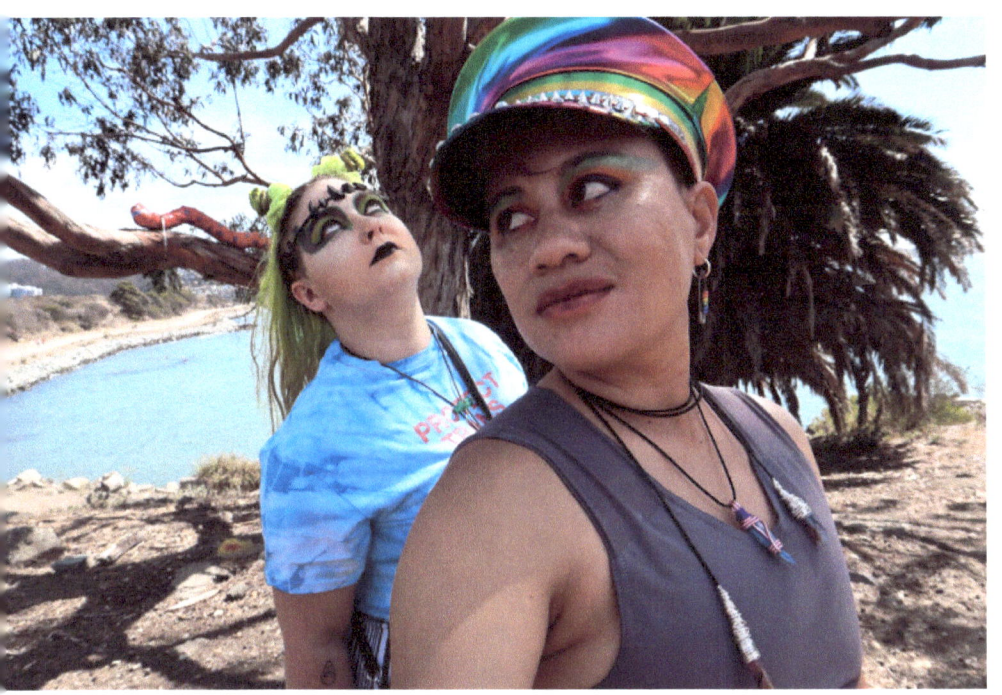

Models left to right: Marisa Wohlschlaeger, Angel Angeles
Protect Trans Kids shirt by The Phluid Project
Head jewelry by moniautumn
Necklace by Spiritually Stoned Co
Lariats by Gemder Fluid Designs

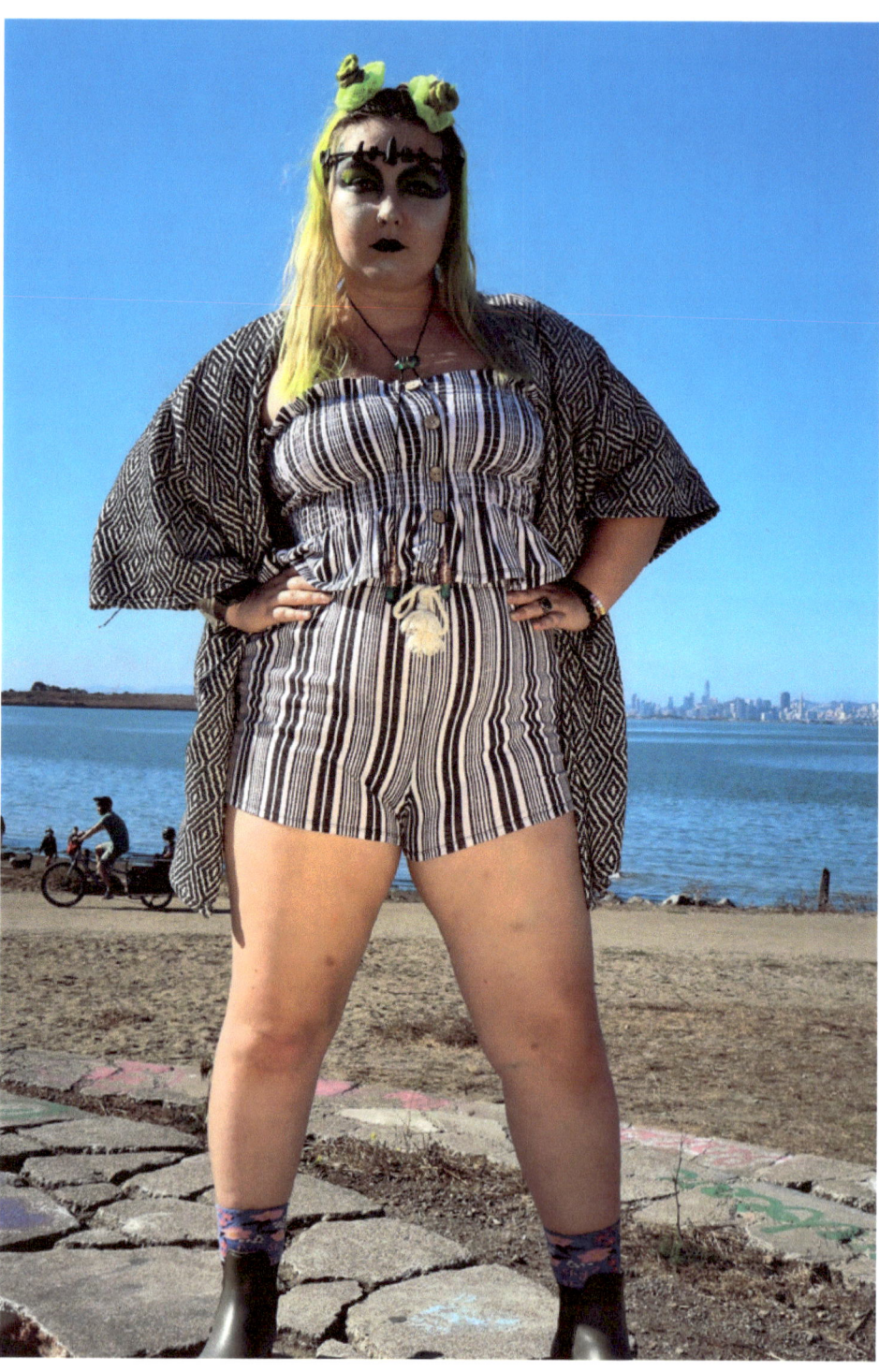

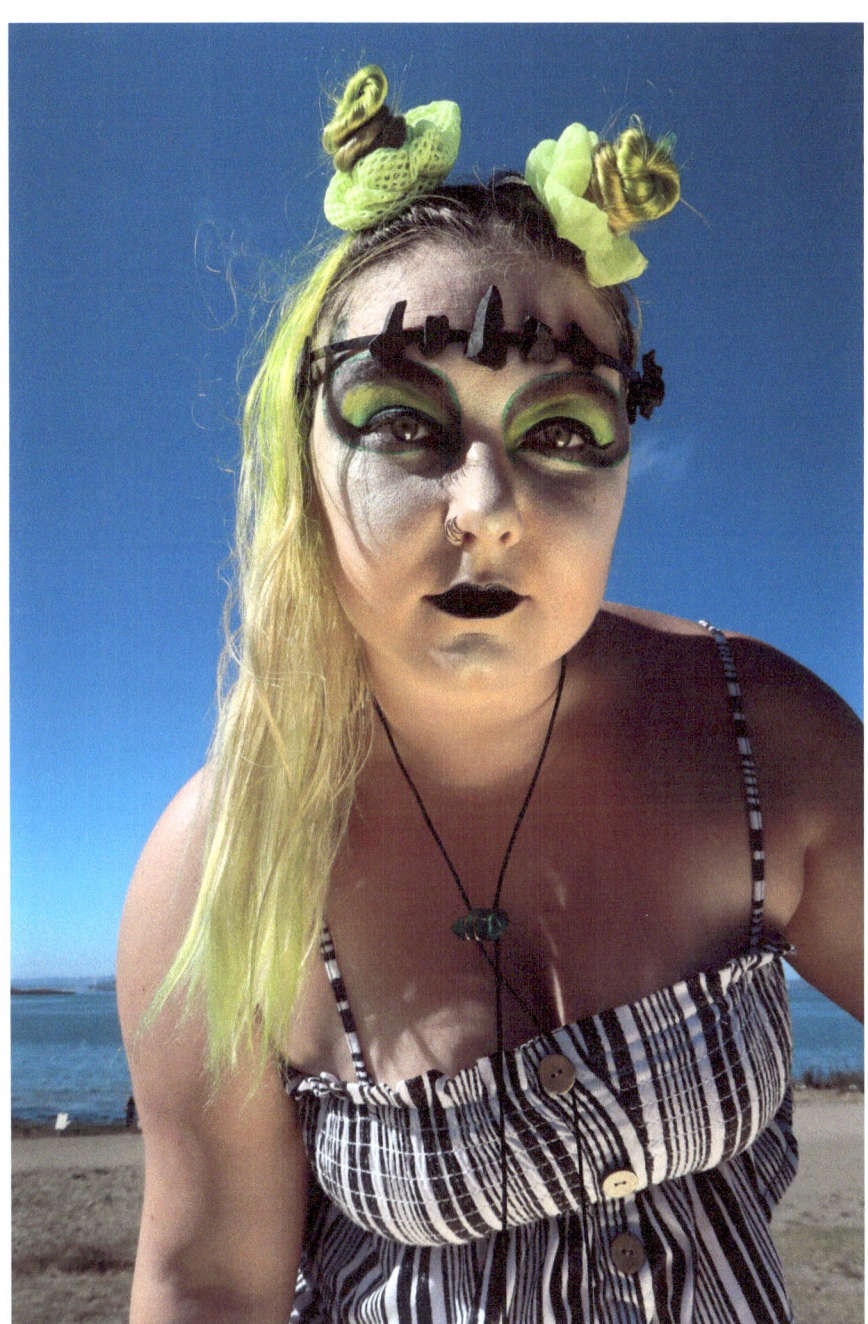

Model: Marisa Wohlschlaeger
Photographer: Angel Angeles
Head jewelry by moniautumn
Lariat by Gemder Fluid Designs

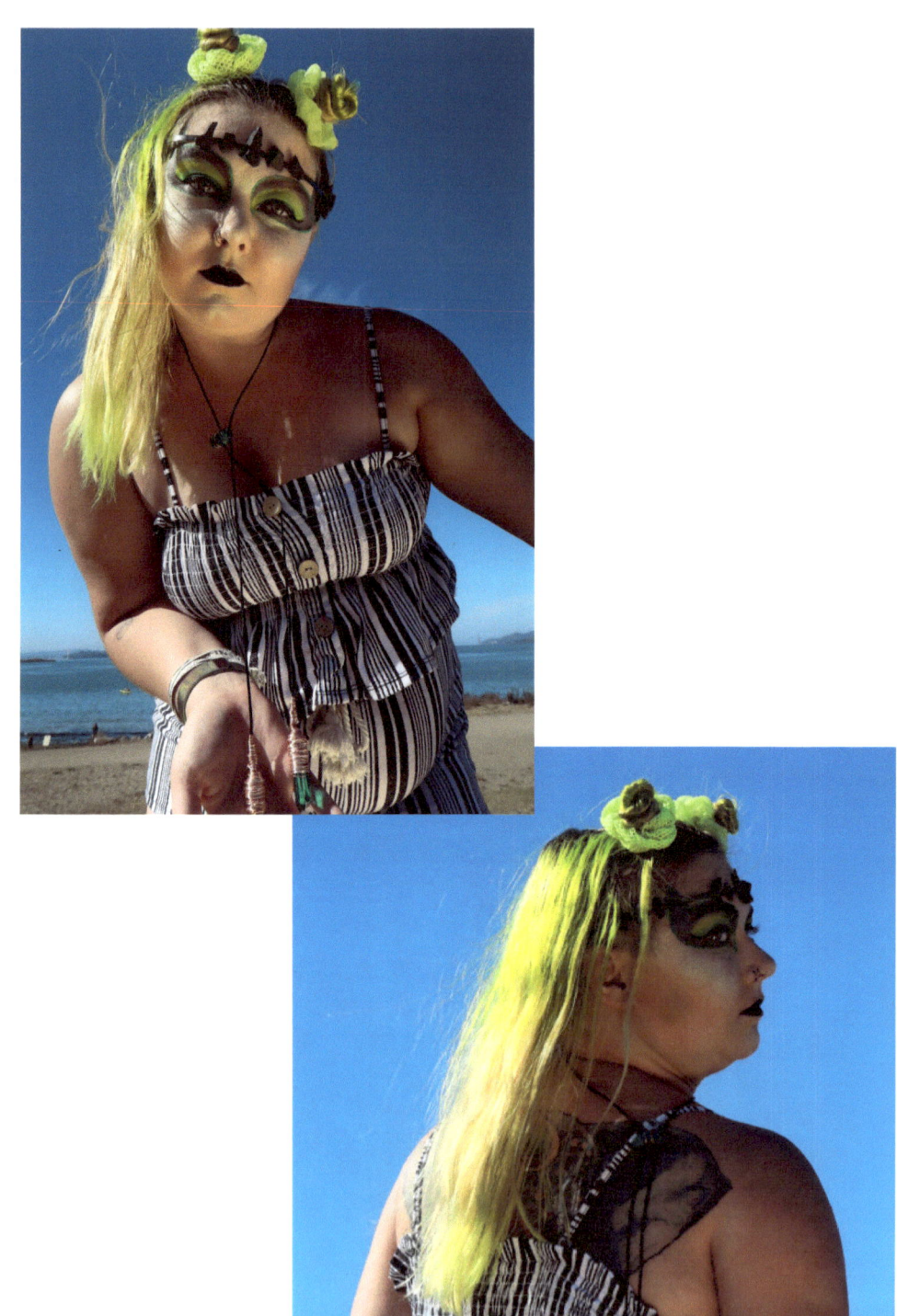

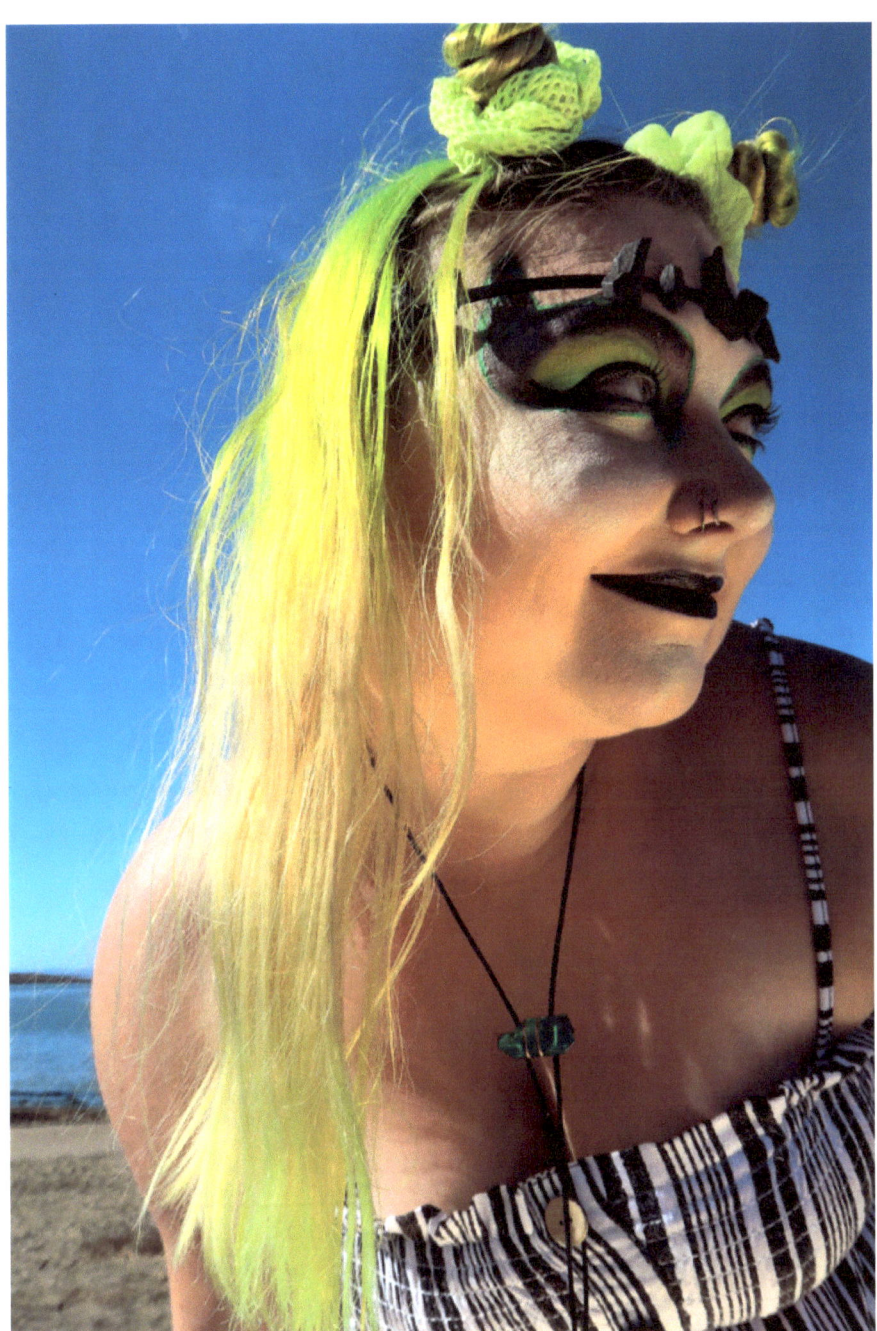

Model: Marisa Wohlschlaeger
Photographer: Angel Angeles
Head jewelry by moniautumn
Lariat by Gemder Fluid Designs

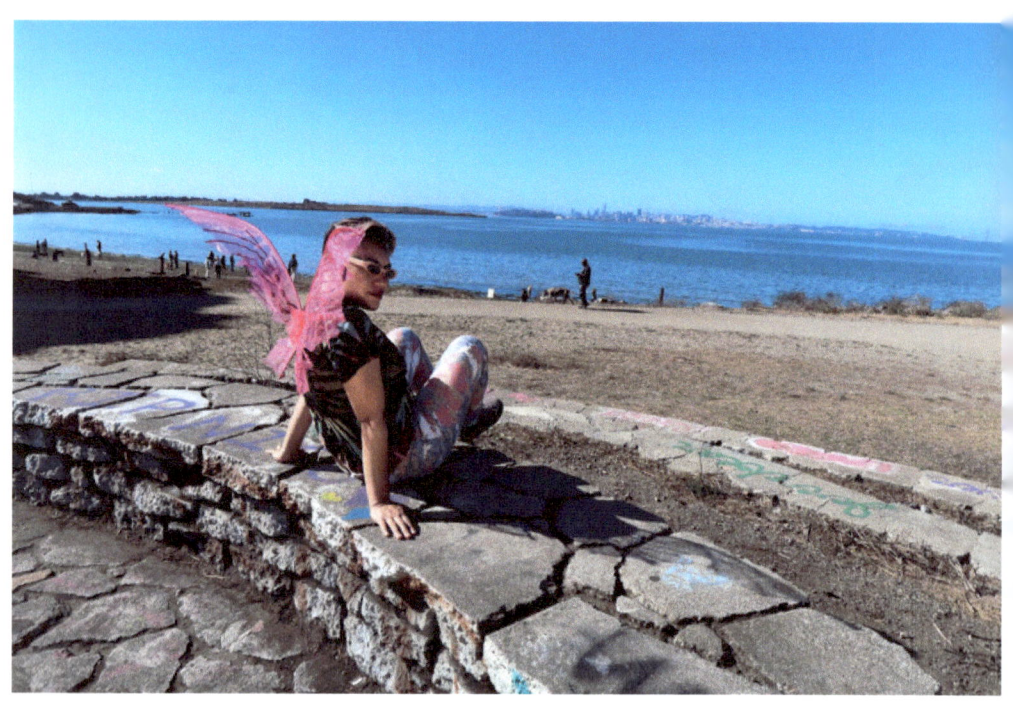

Model: Angel Angeles
Photographer: Marisa Wohlschlaeger
Shop Local Queer BIPOC shirt by The Phluid Project
Necklace by Spiritually Stoned Co
Lariat by Gemder Fluid Designs

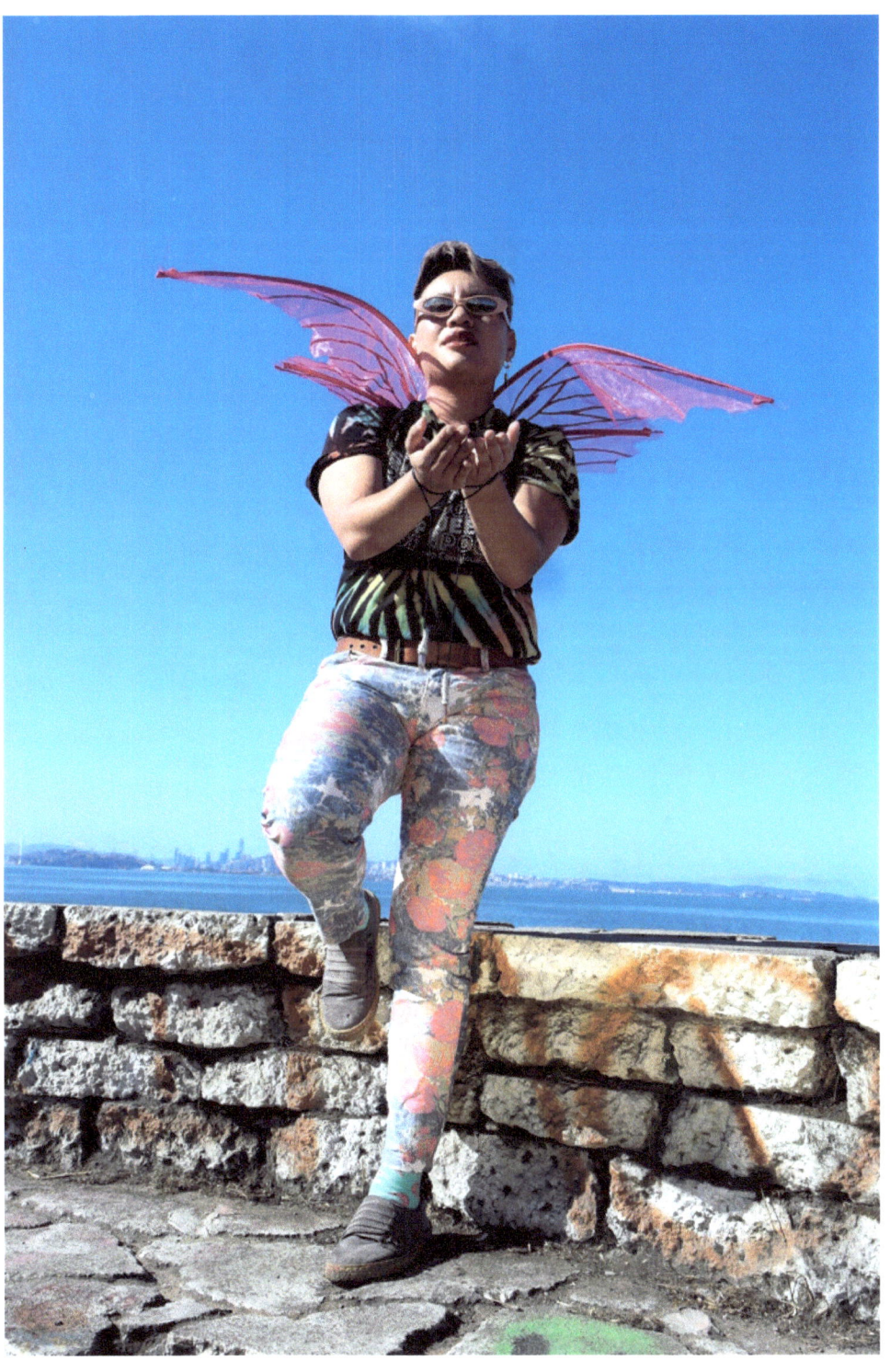

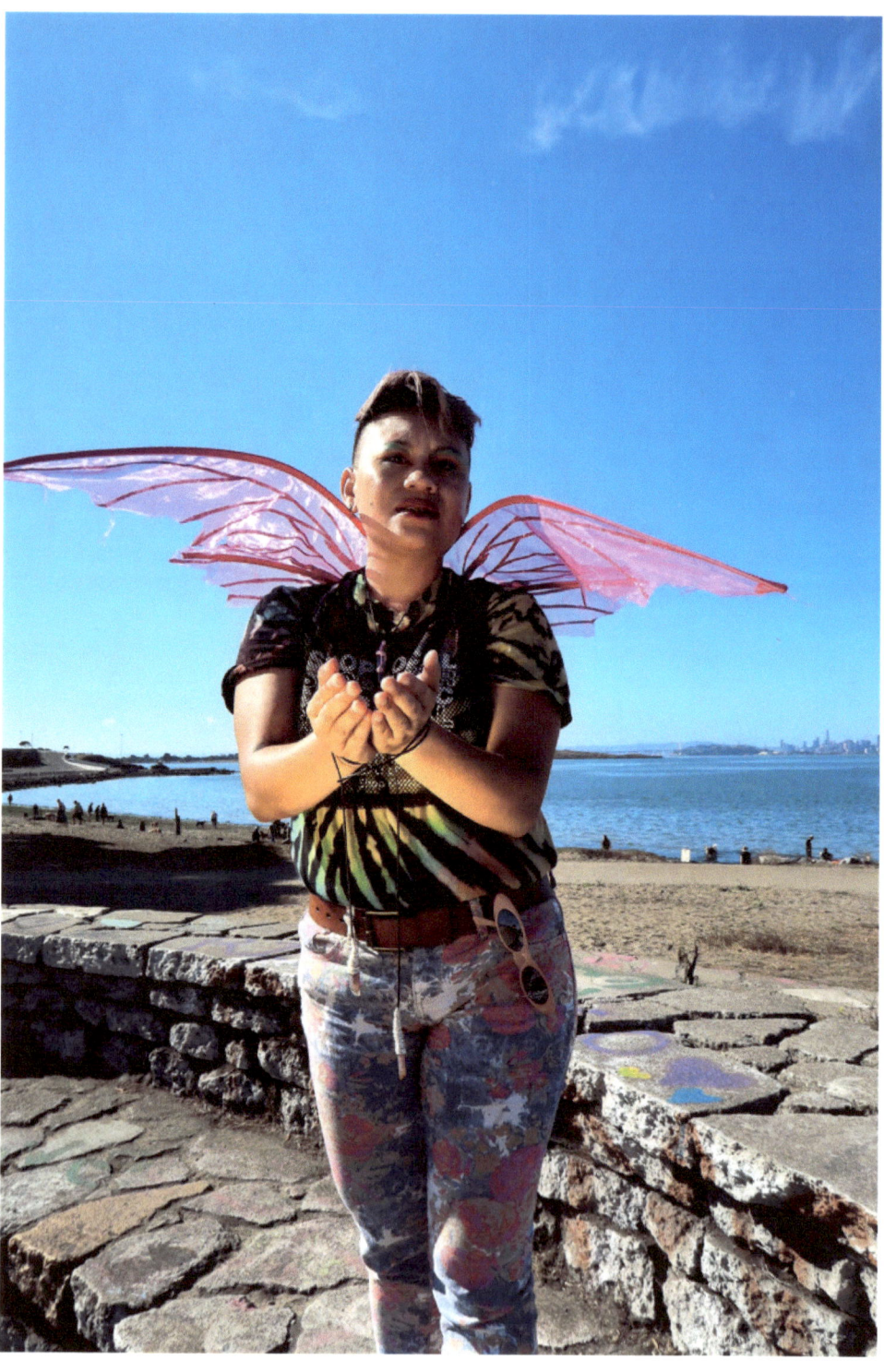

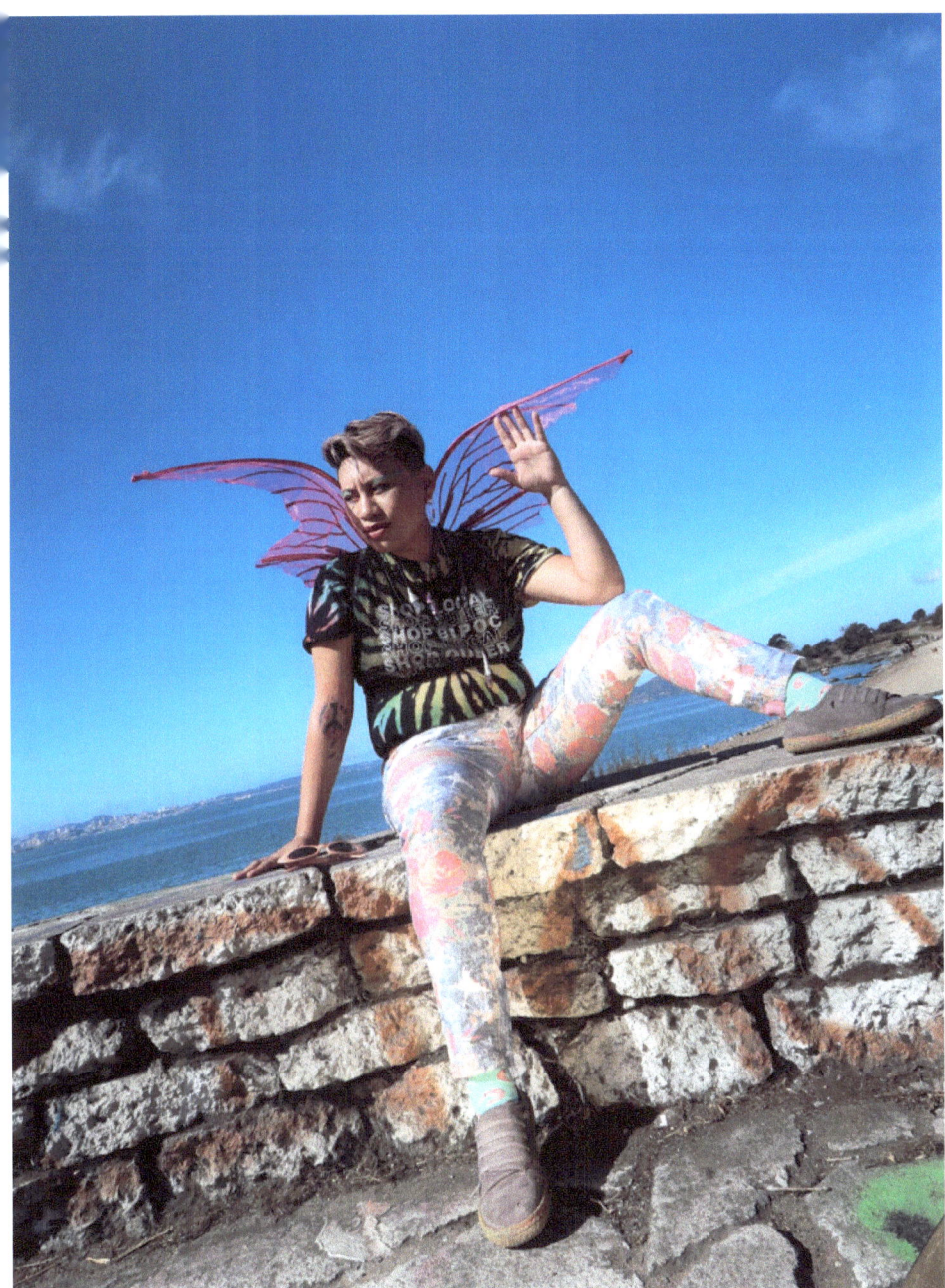

Model: Angel Angeles
Photographer: Marisa Wohlschlaeger
Shop Local Queer BIPOC shirt by The Phluid Project
Necklace by Spiritually Stoned Co
Lariat by Gemder Fluid Designs

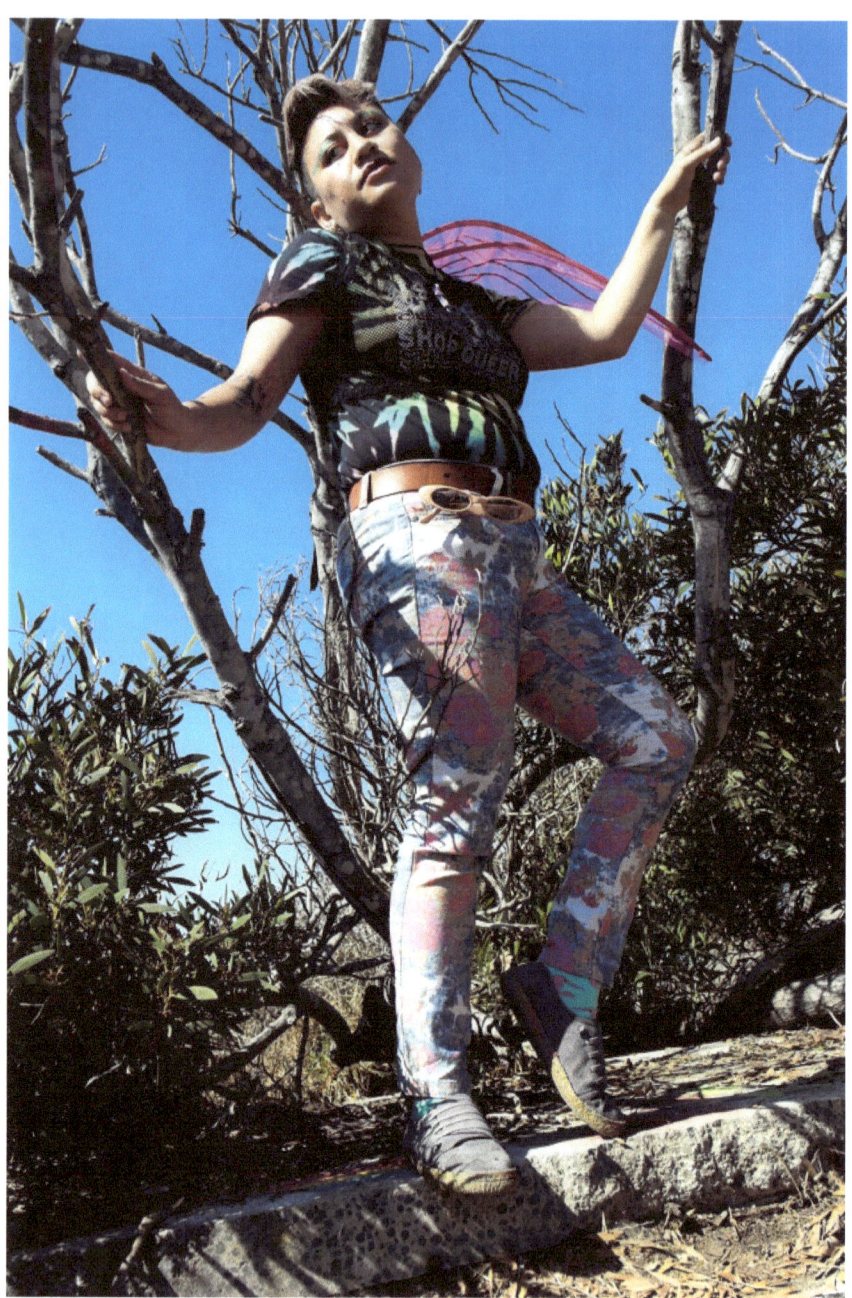

Model: Angel Angeles
Photographer: Marisa Wohlschlaeger
Shop Local Queer BIPOC shirt by The Phluid Project
Necklace by Spiritually Stoned Co
Lariat by Gemder Fluid Designs

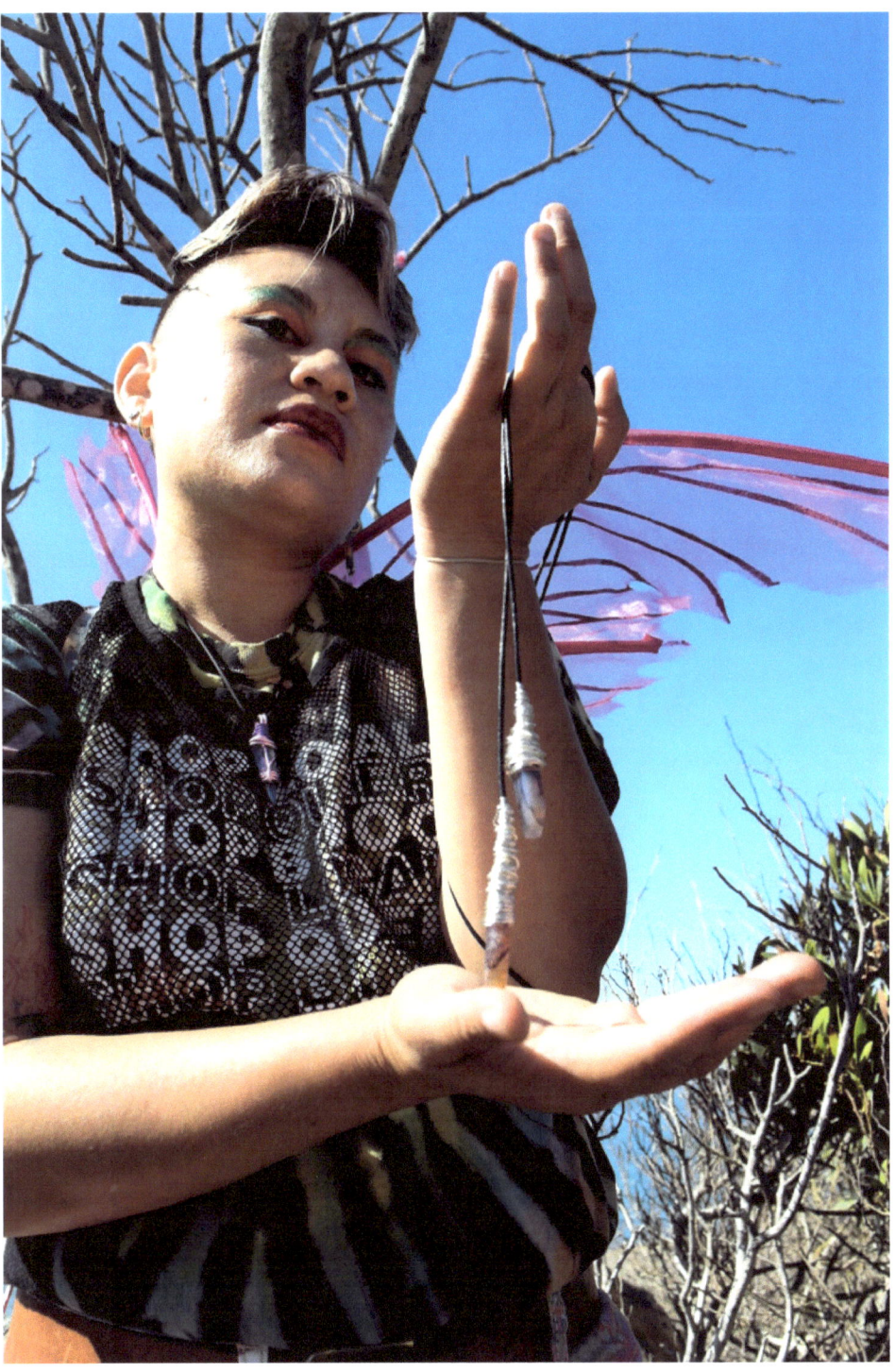

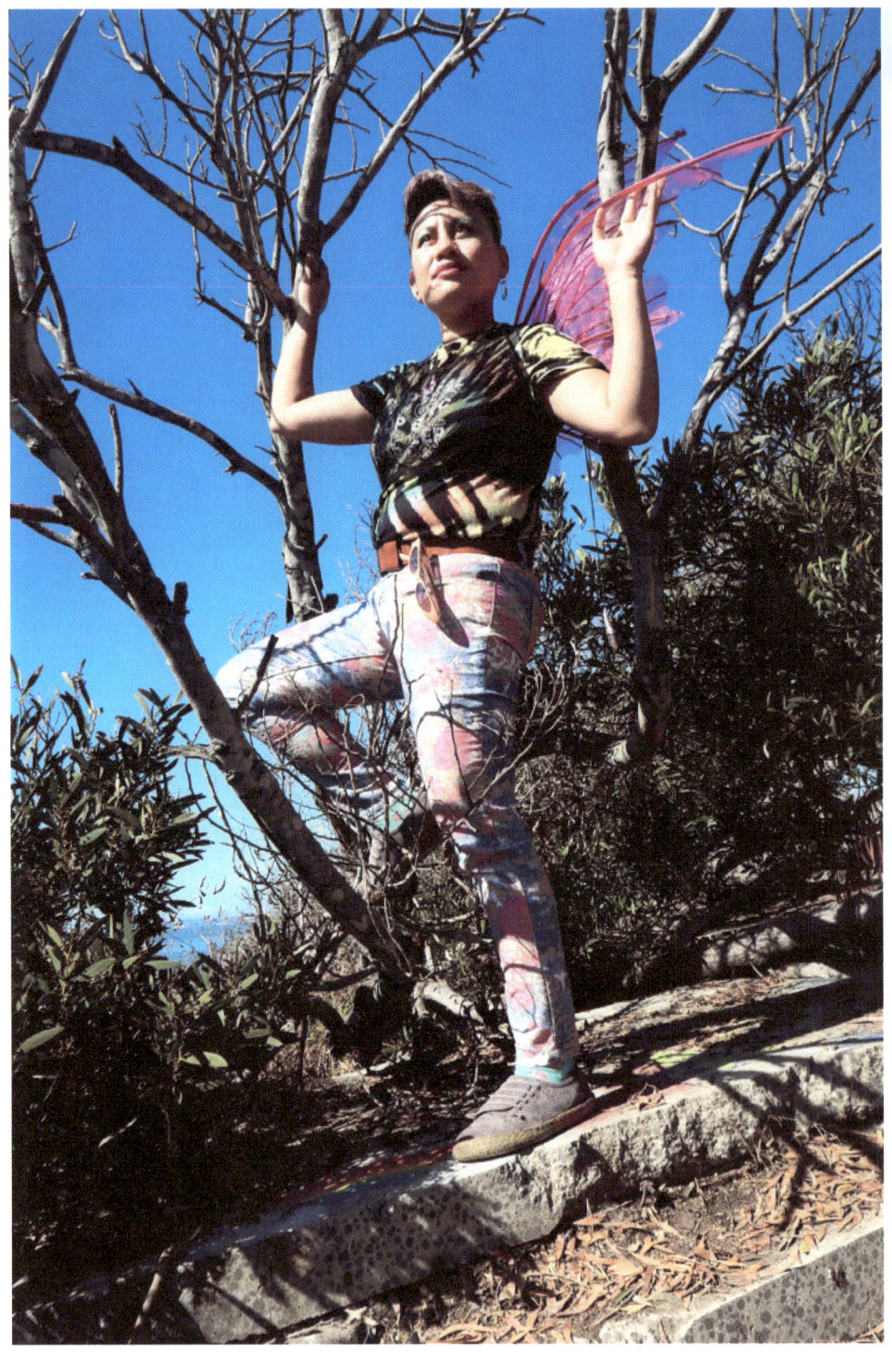

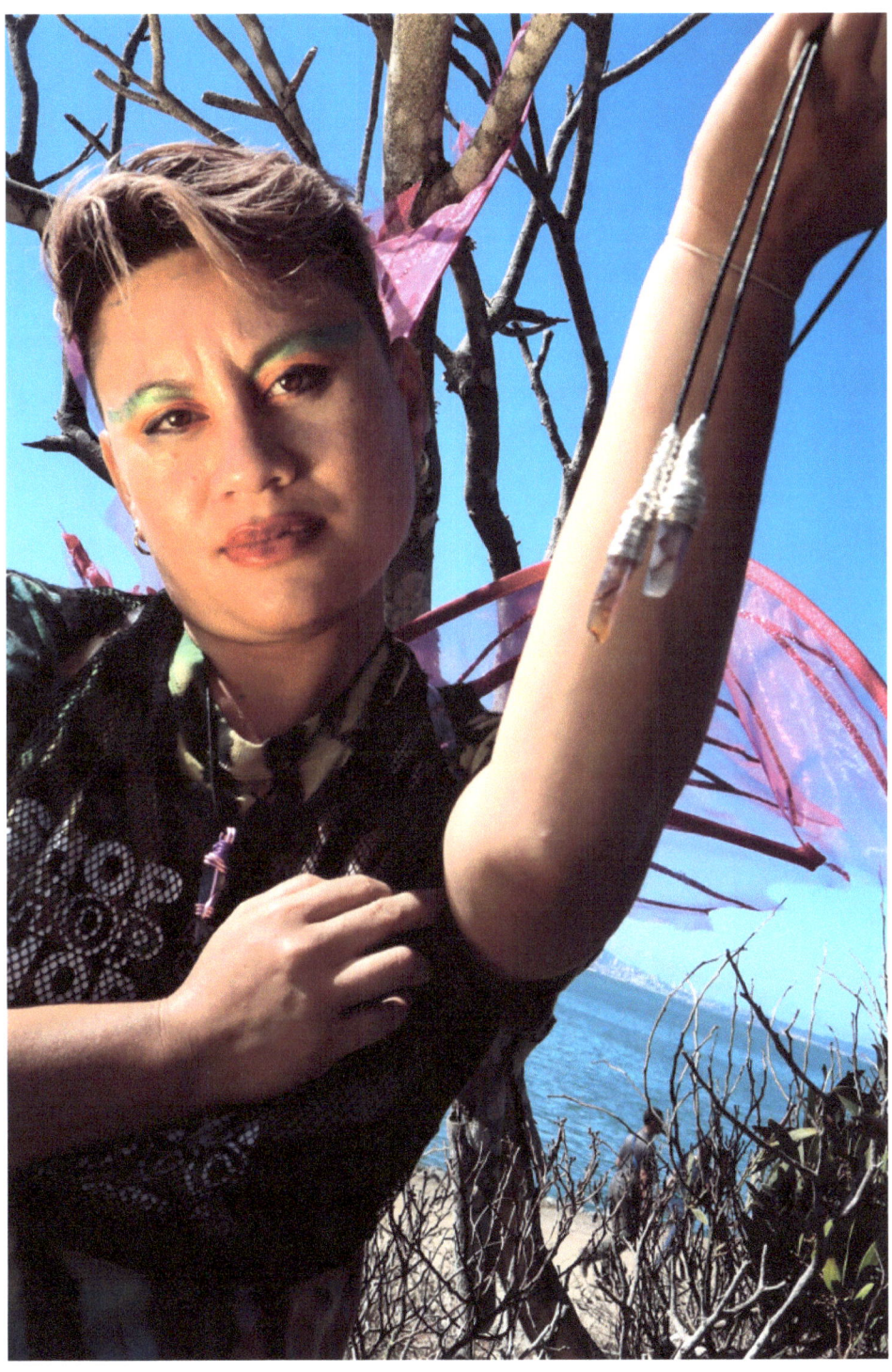

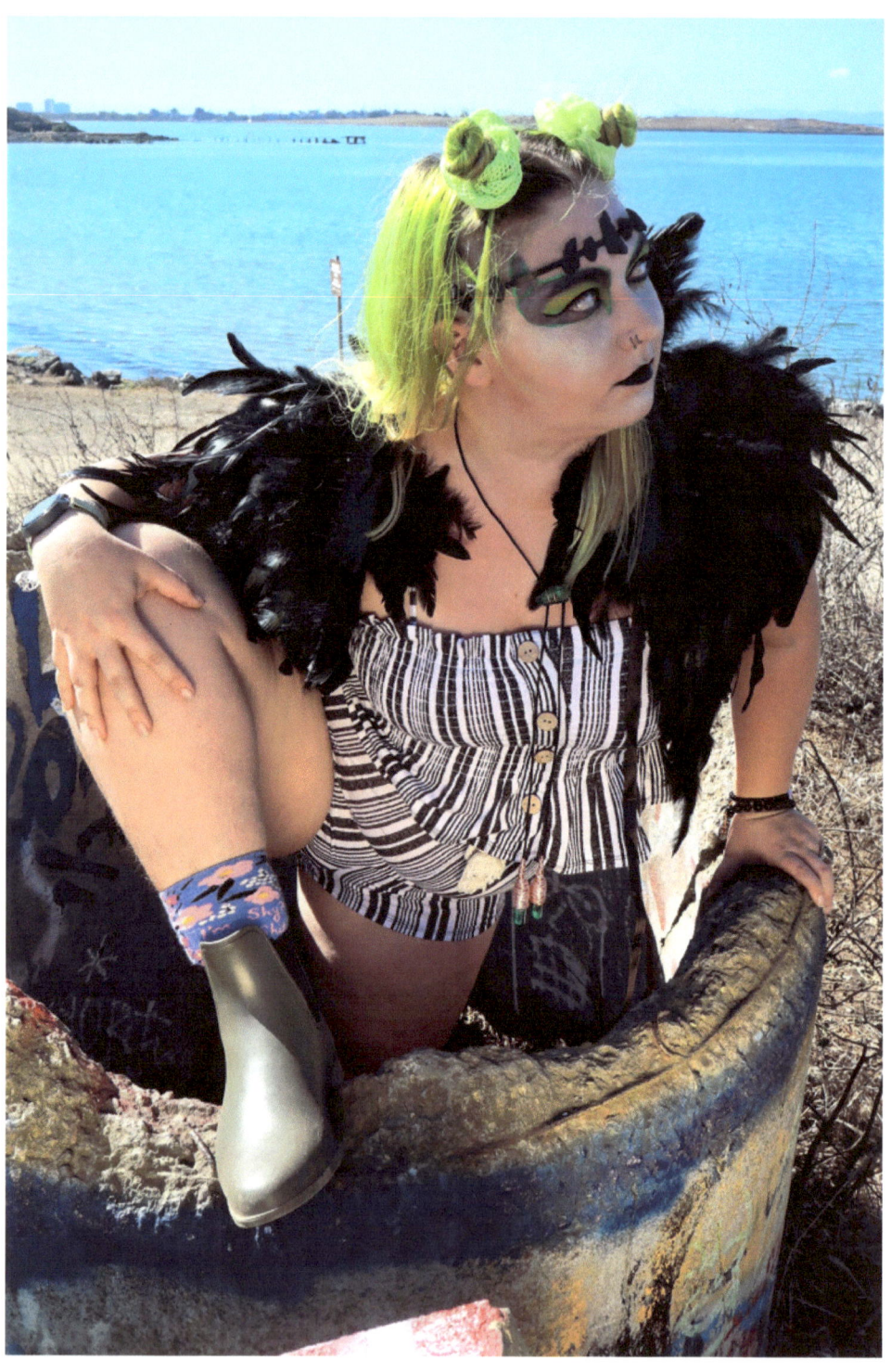

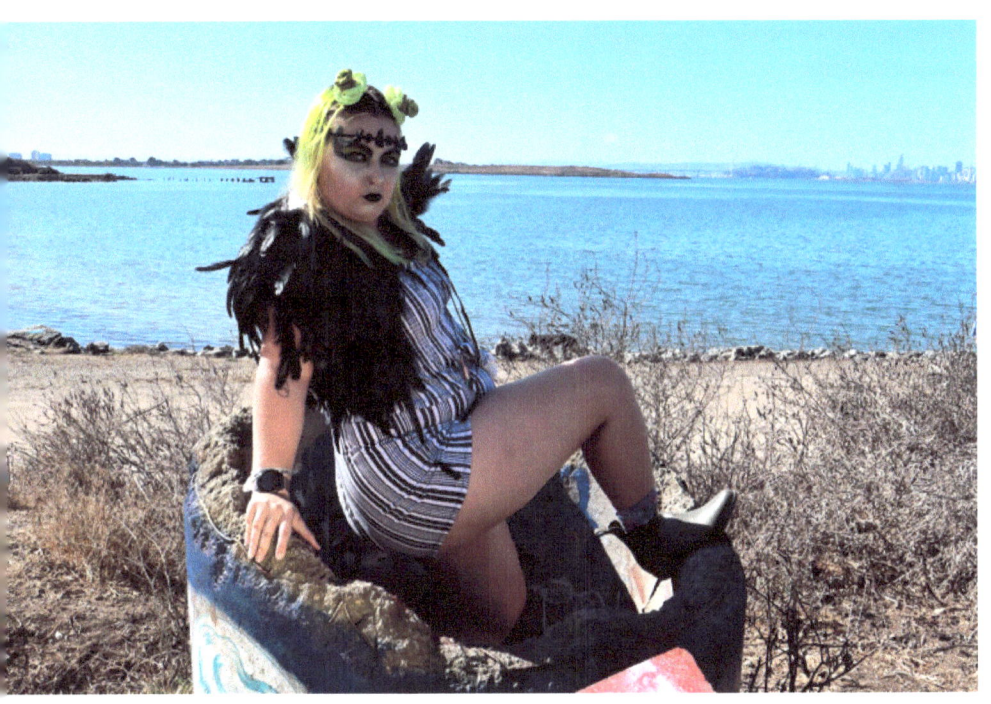

Model: Marisa Wohlschlaeger
Photographer: Angel Angeles
Head jewelry by moniautumn
Lariat by Gemder Fluid Designs

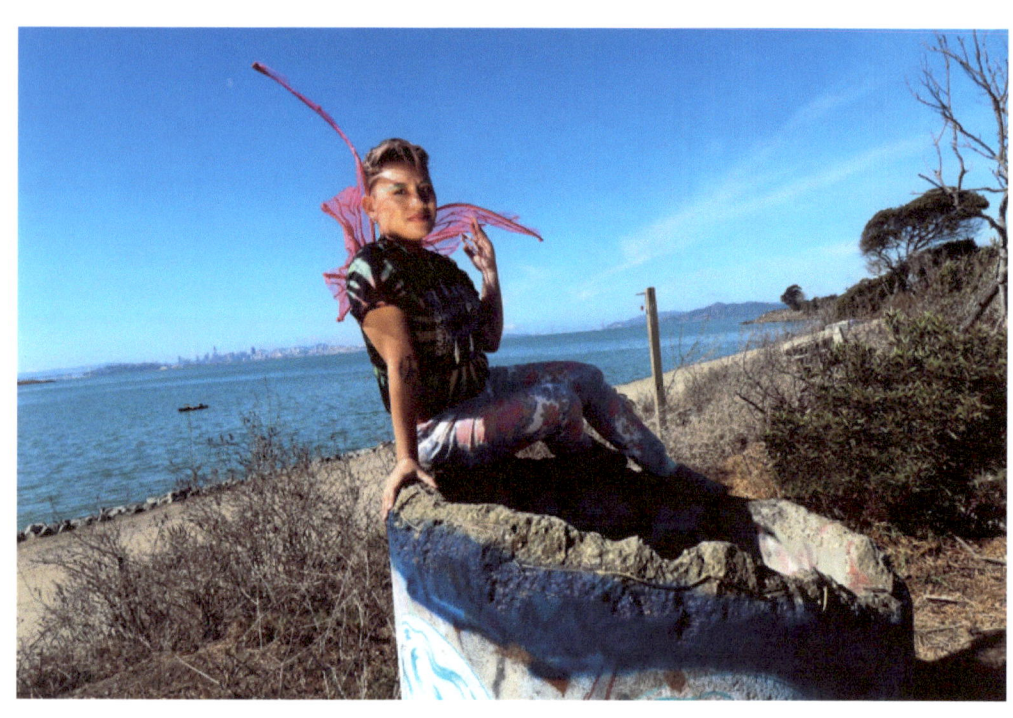

Model: Angel Angeles
Photographer: Marisa Wohlschlaeger
Shop Local Queer BIPOC shirt by The Phluid Project
Necklace by Spiritually Stoned Co
Lariat by Gemder Fluid Designs

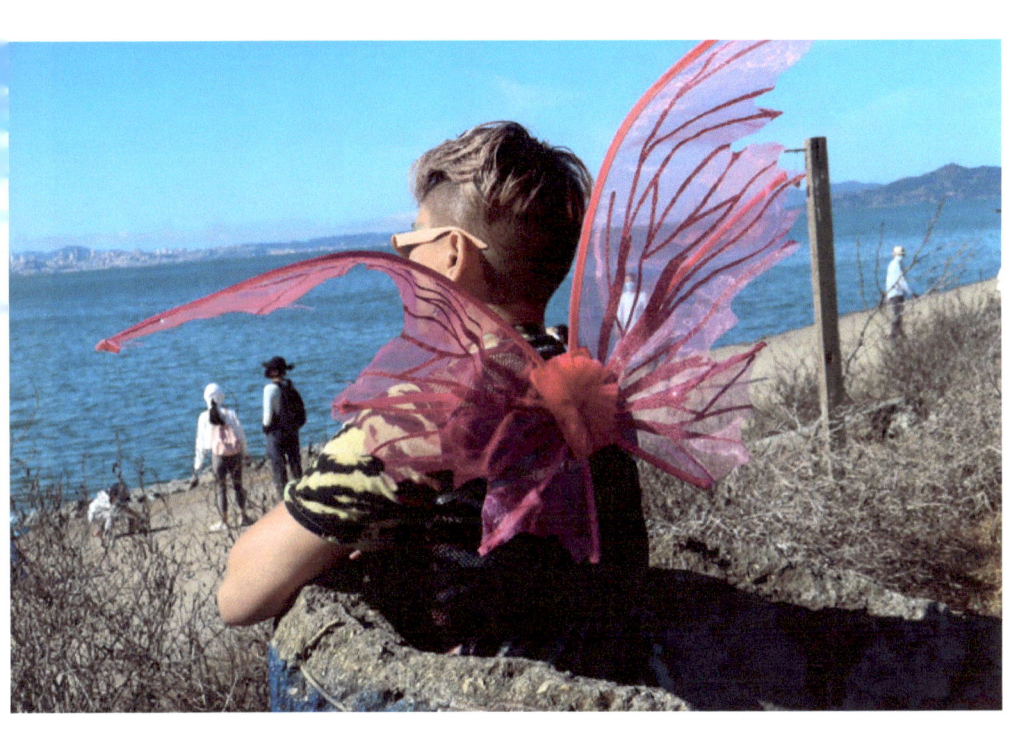

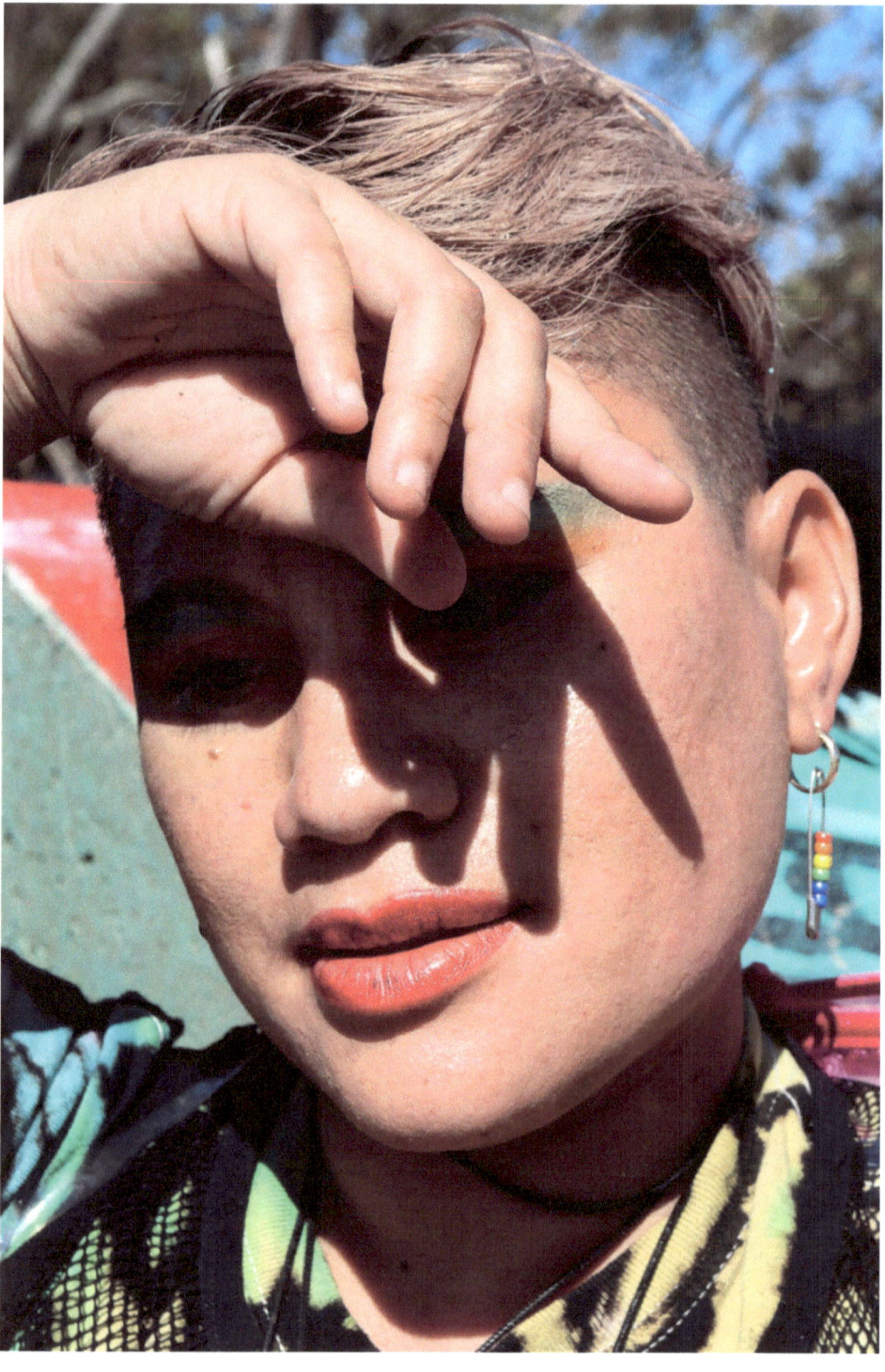

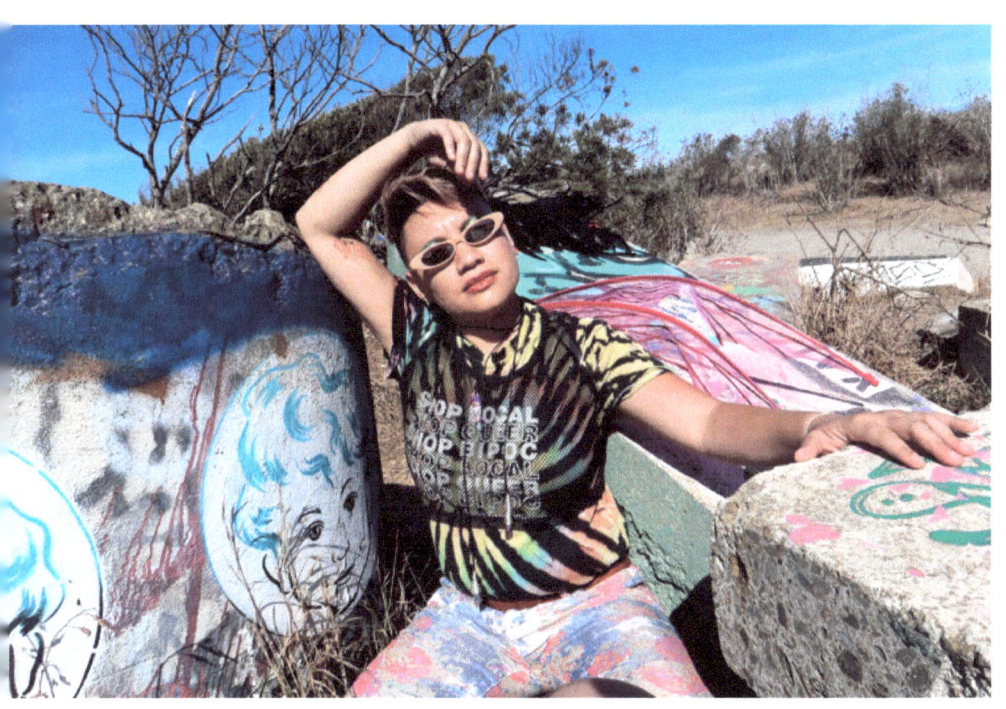

Model: Angel Angeles
Photographer: Marisa Wohlschlaeger
Shop Local Queer BIPOC shirt by The Phluid Project
Necklace by Spiritually Stoned Co
Lariat by Gemder Fluid Designs

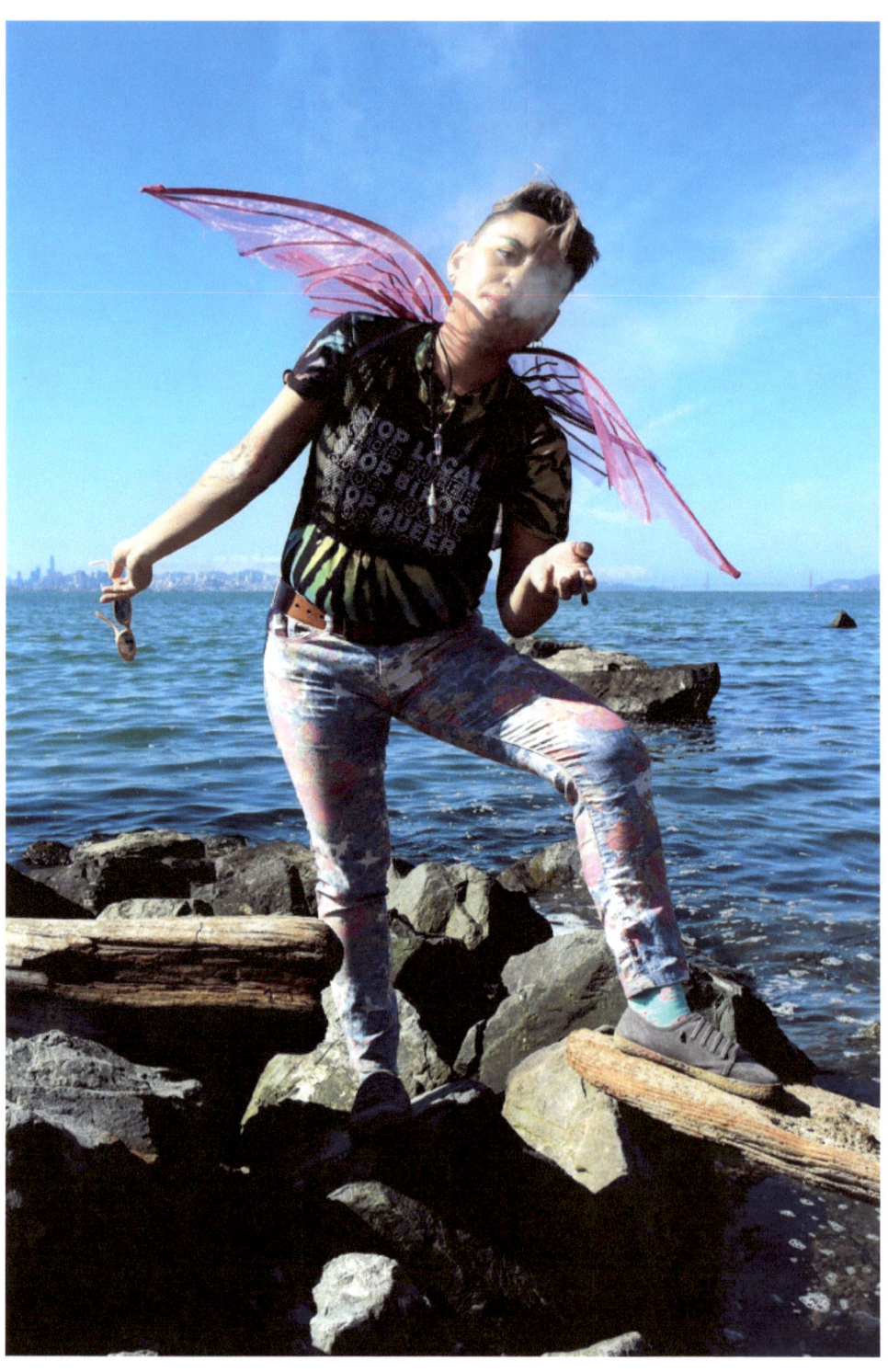

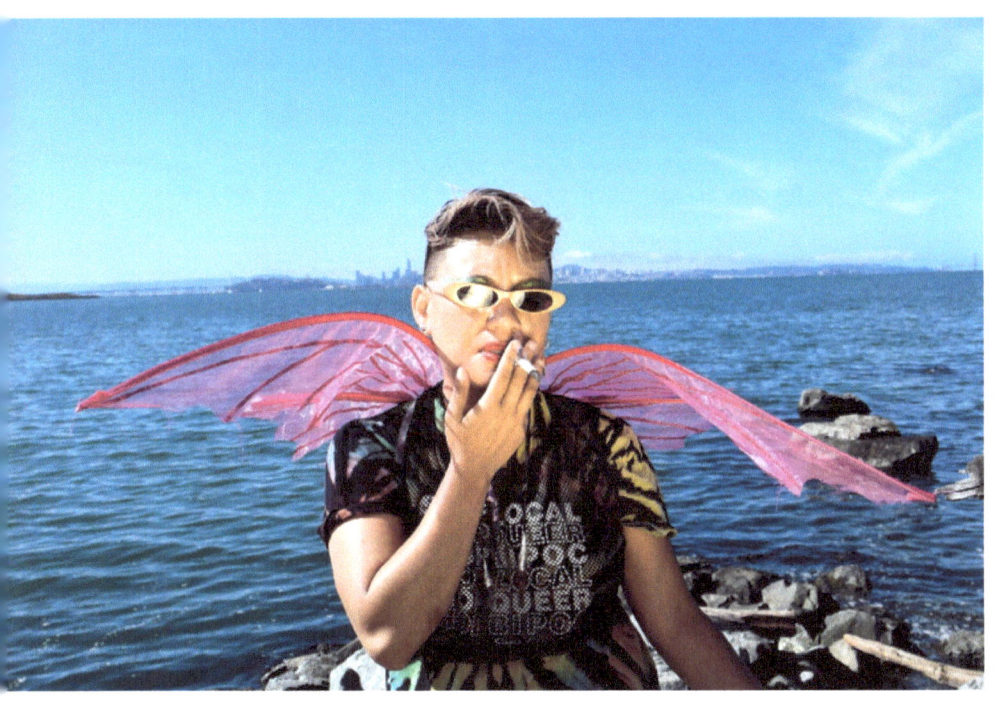

Model: Angel Angeles
Photographer: Marisa Wohlschlaeger
Shop Local Queer BIPOC shirt by The Phluid Project
Necklace by Spiritually Stoned Co
Lariat by Gemder Fluid Designs

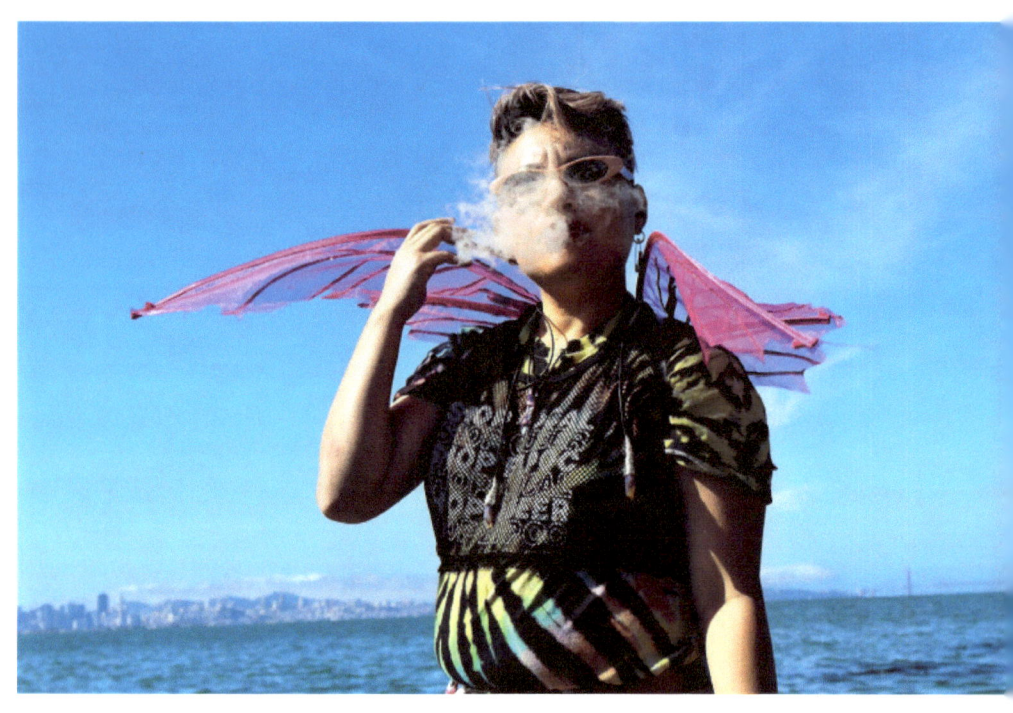

Model: Angel Angeles
Photographer: Marisa Wohlschlaeger
Shop Local Queer BIPOC shirt by The Phluid Project
Necklace by Spiritually Stoned Co
Lariat by Gemder Fluid Designs

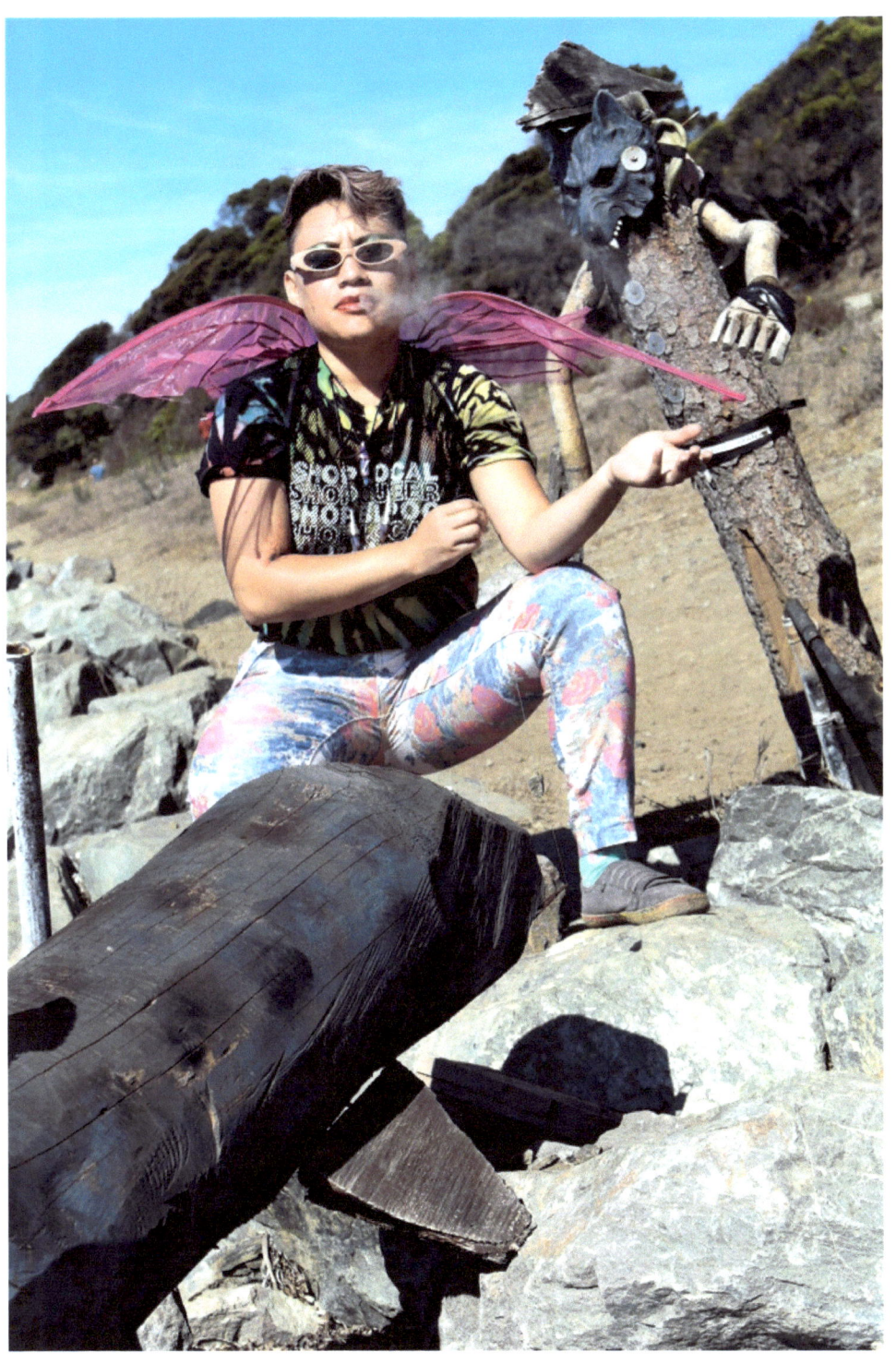

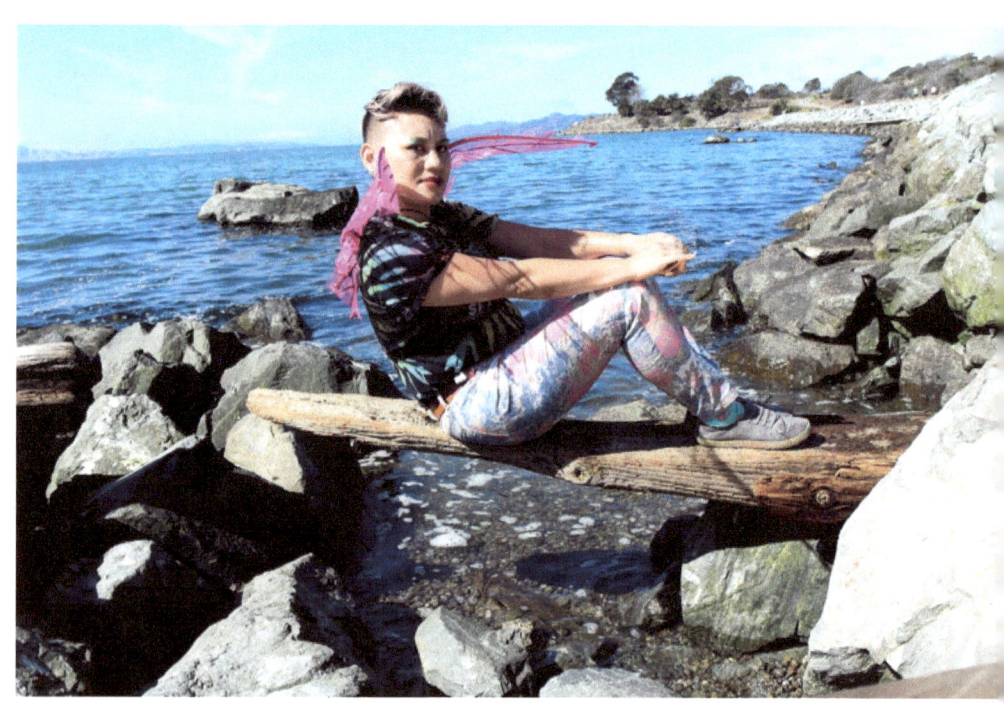

Model: Angel Angeles
Photographer: Marisa Wohlschlaeger
Shop Local Queer BIPOC shirt by The Phluid Project
Necklace by Spiritually Stoned Co
Lariat by Gemder Fluid Designs

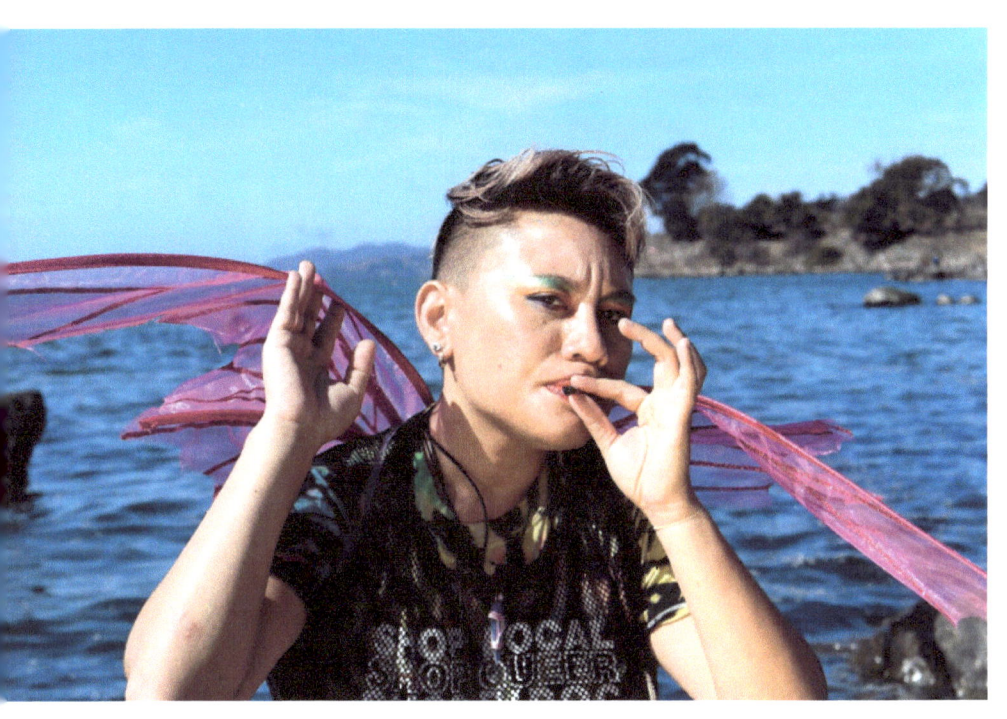

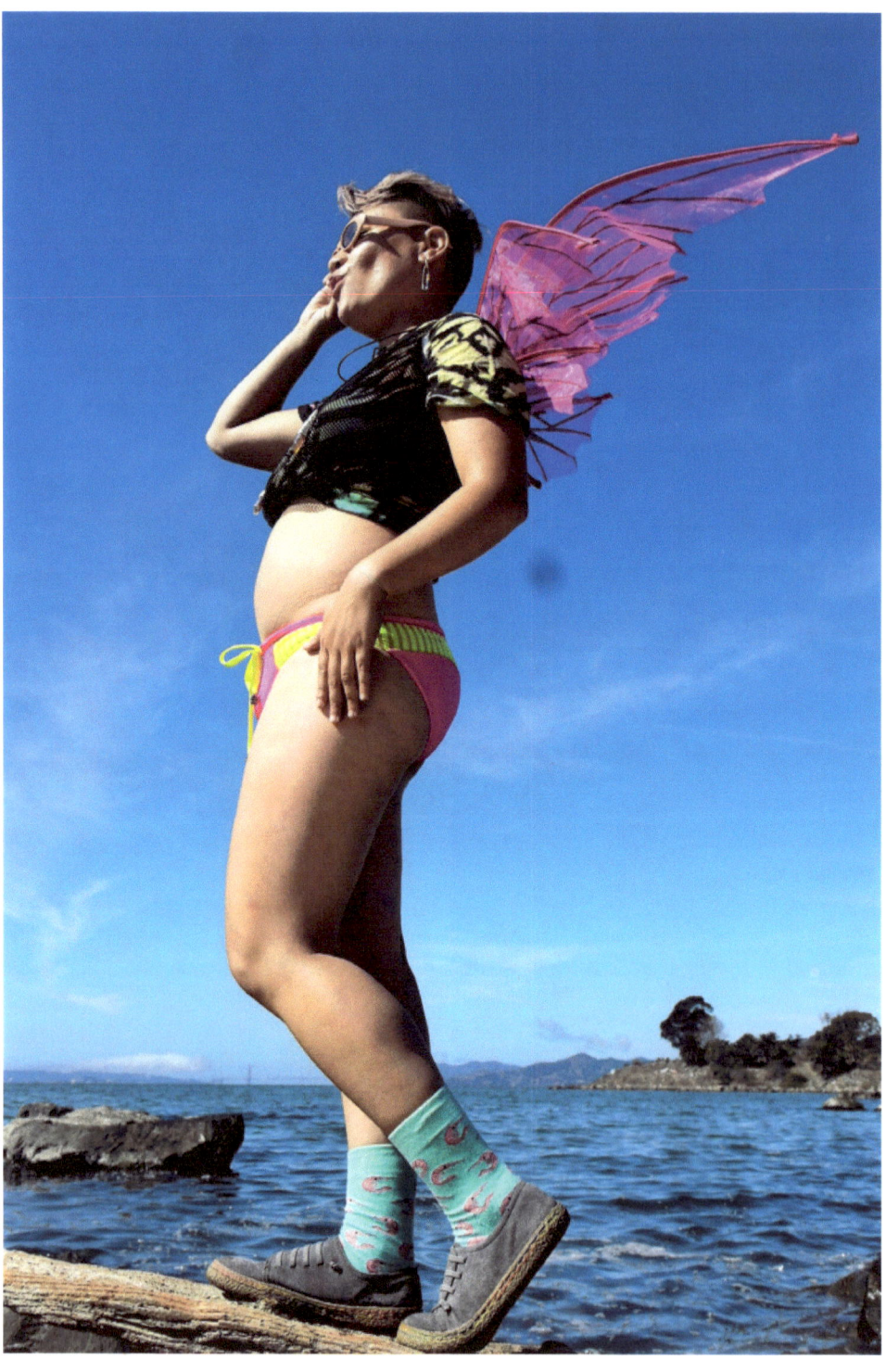

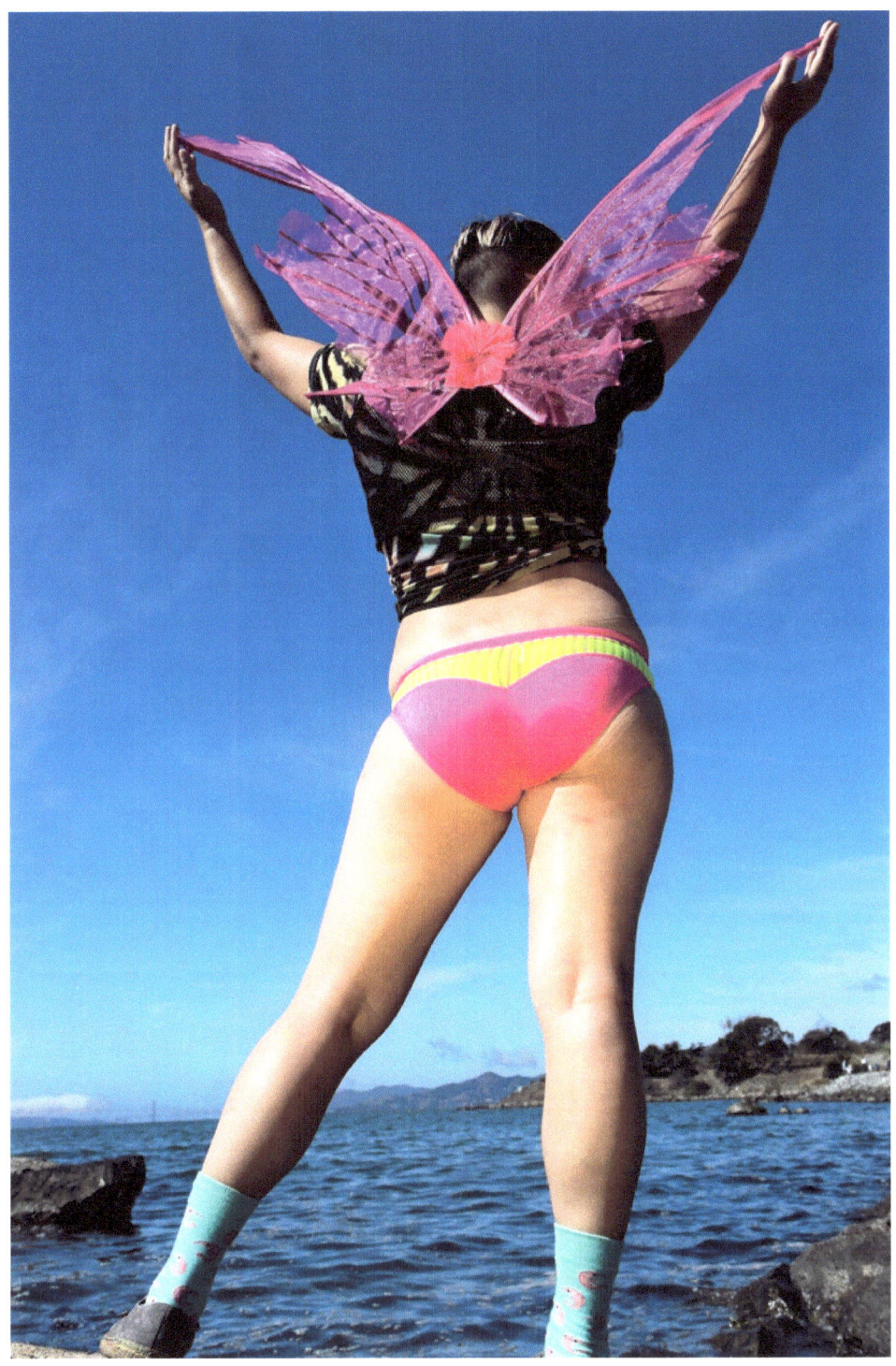

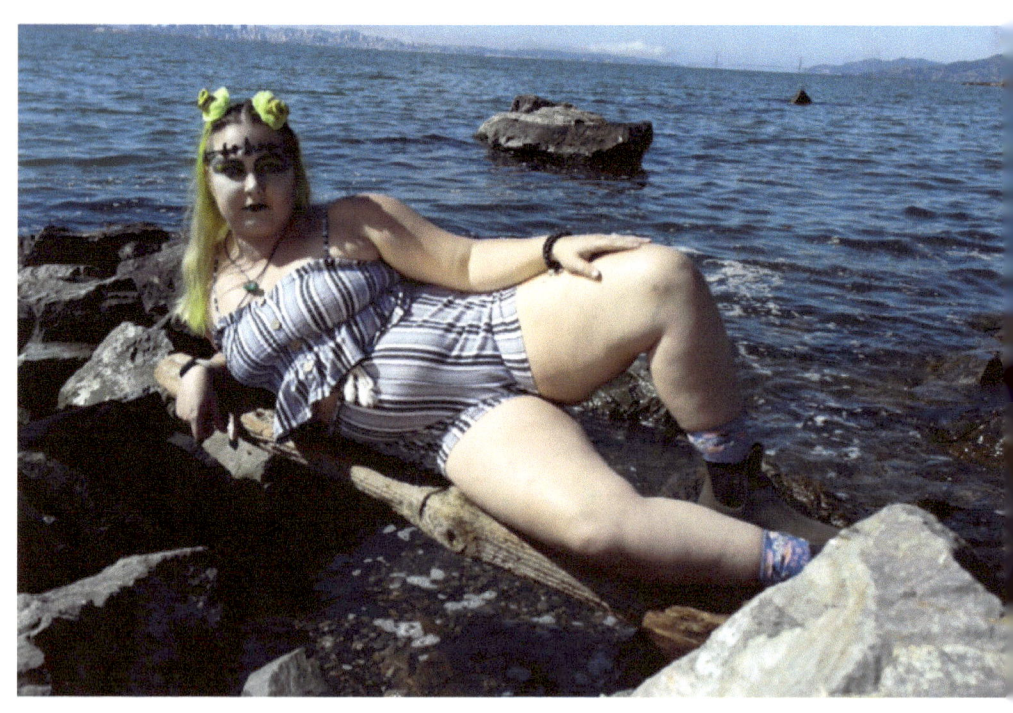

Model: Marisa Wohlschlaeger
Photographer: Angel Angeles
Head jewelry by moniautumn
Lariat by Gemder Fluid Designs

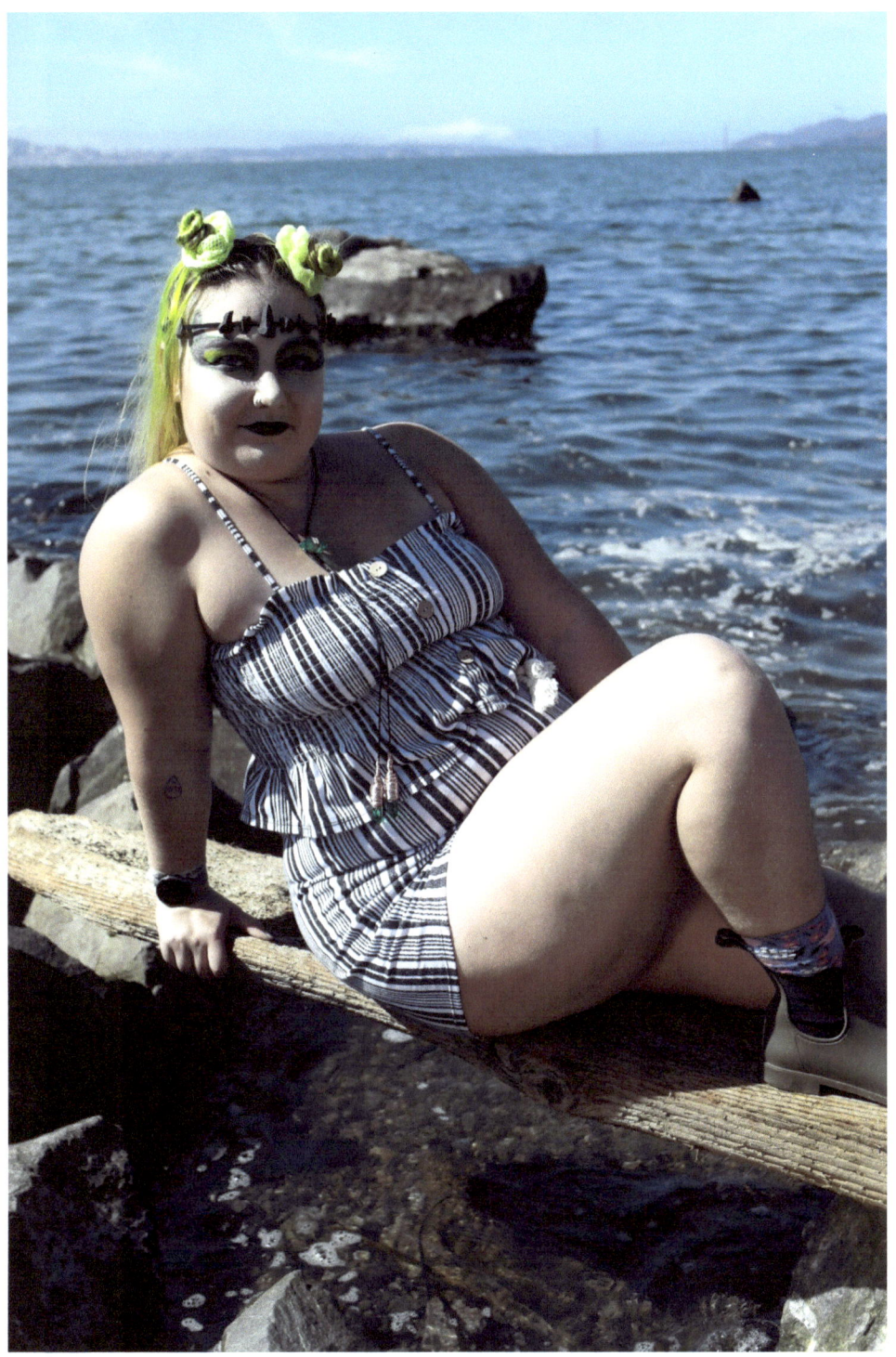

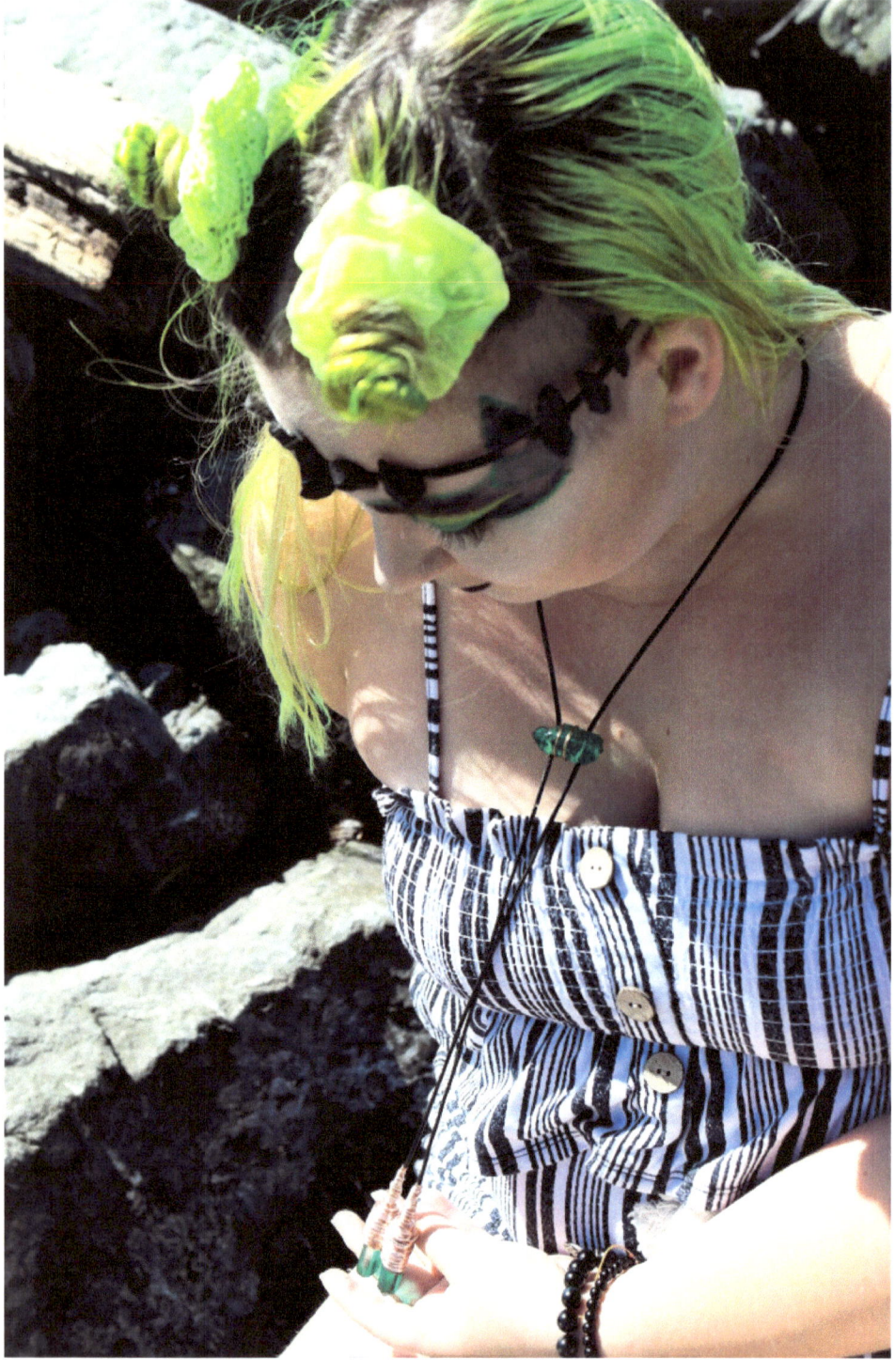

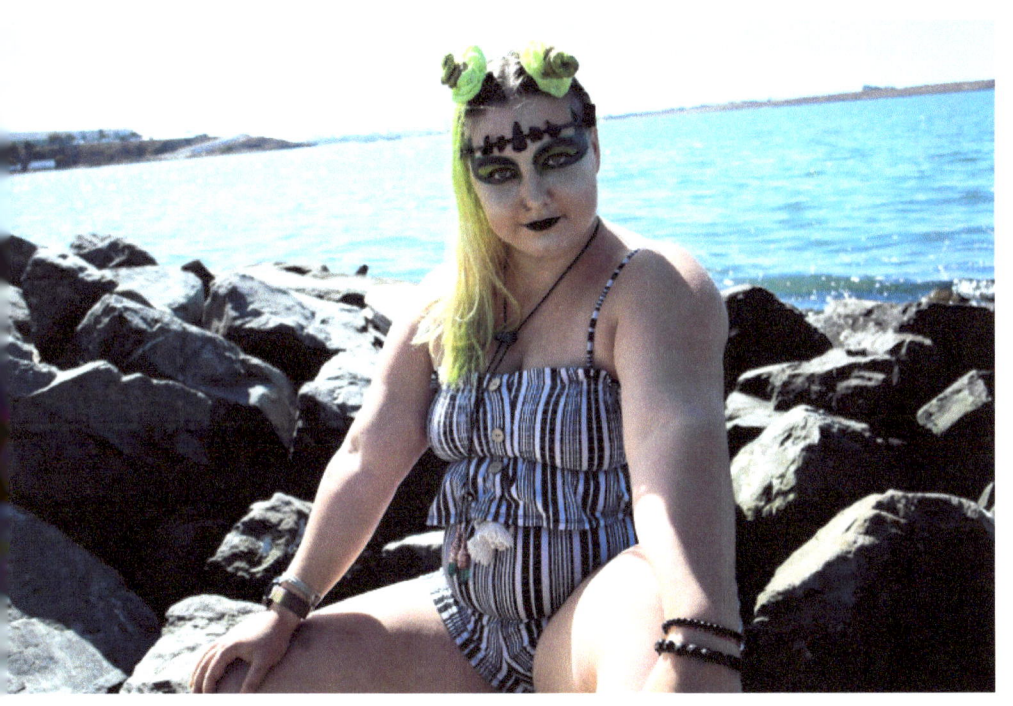

Model: Marisa Wohlschlaeger
Photographer: Angel Angeles
Head jewelry by moniautumn
Lariat by Gemder Fluid Designs

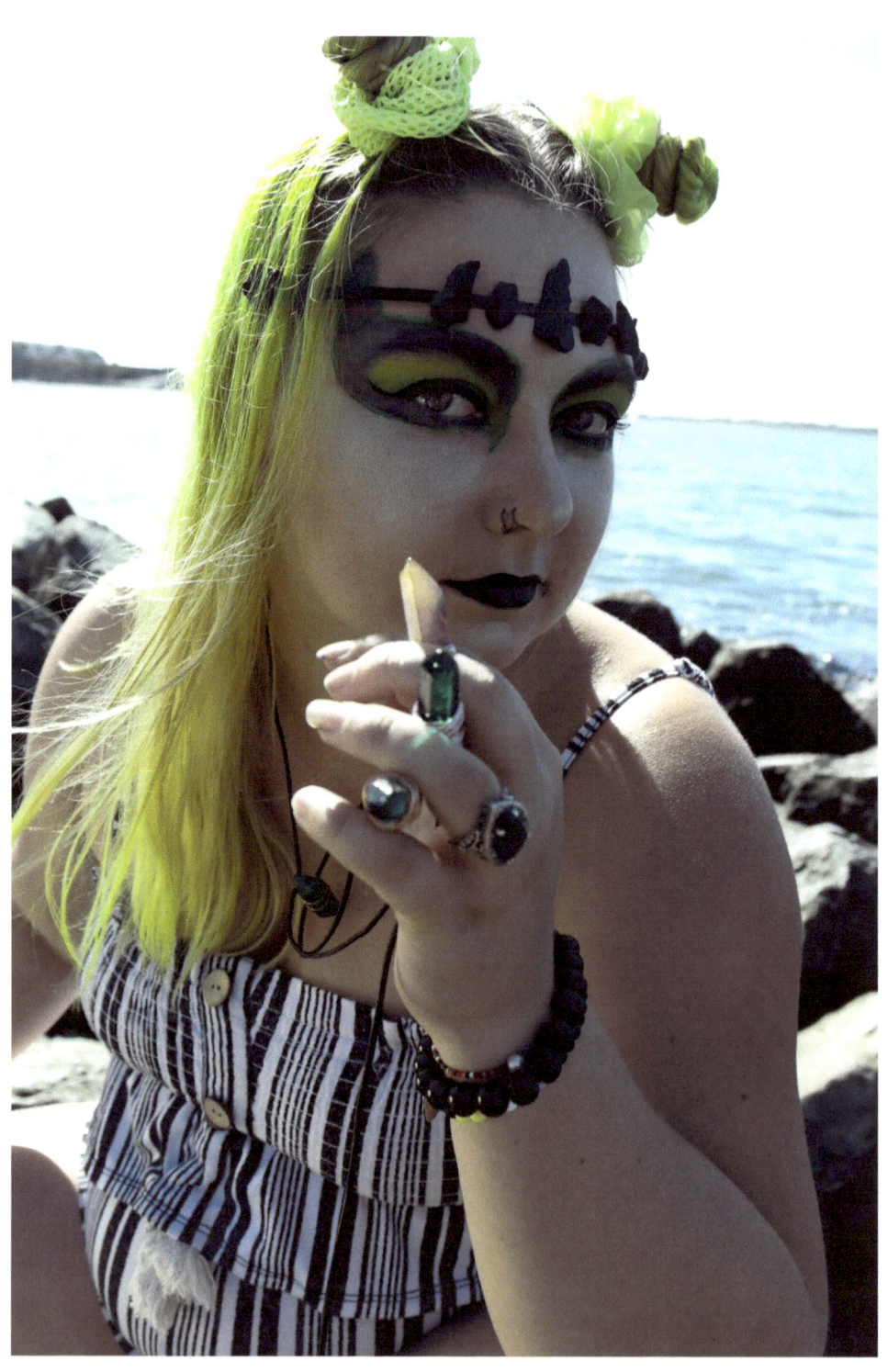

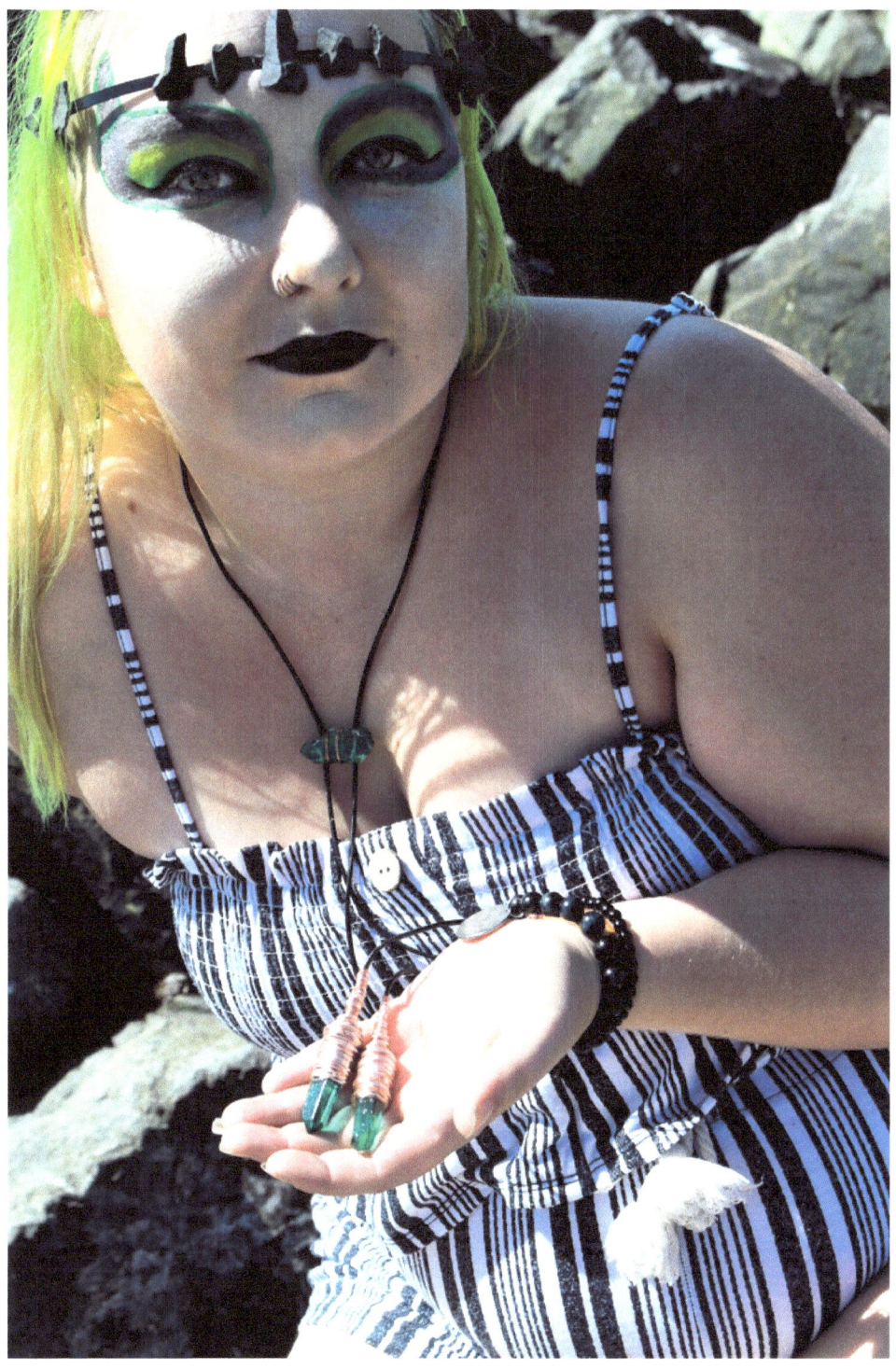

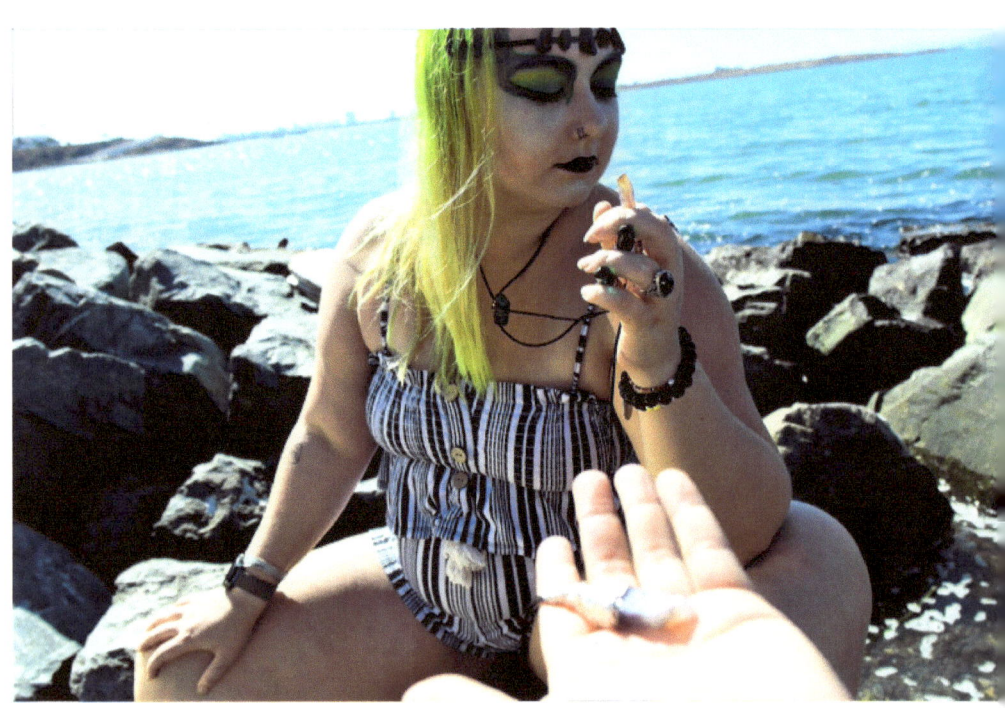

Model: Marisa Wohlschlaeger
Photographer: Angel Angeles
Head jewelry by moniautumn
Lariat by Gemder Fluid Designs

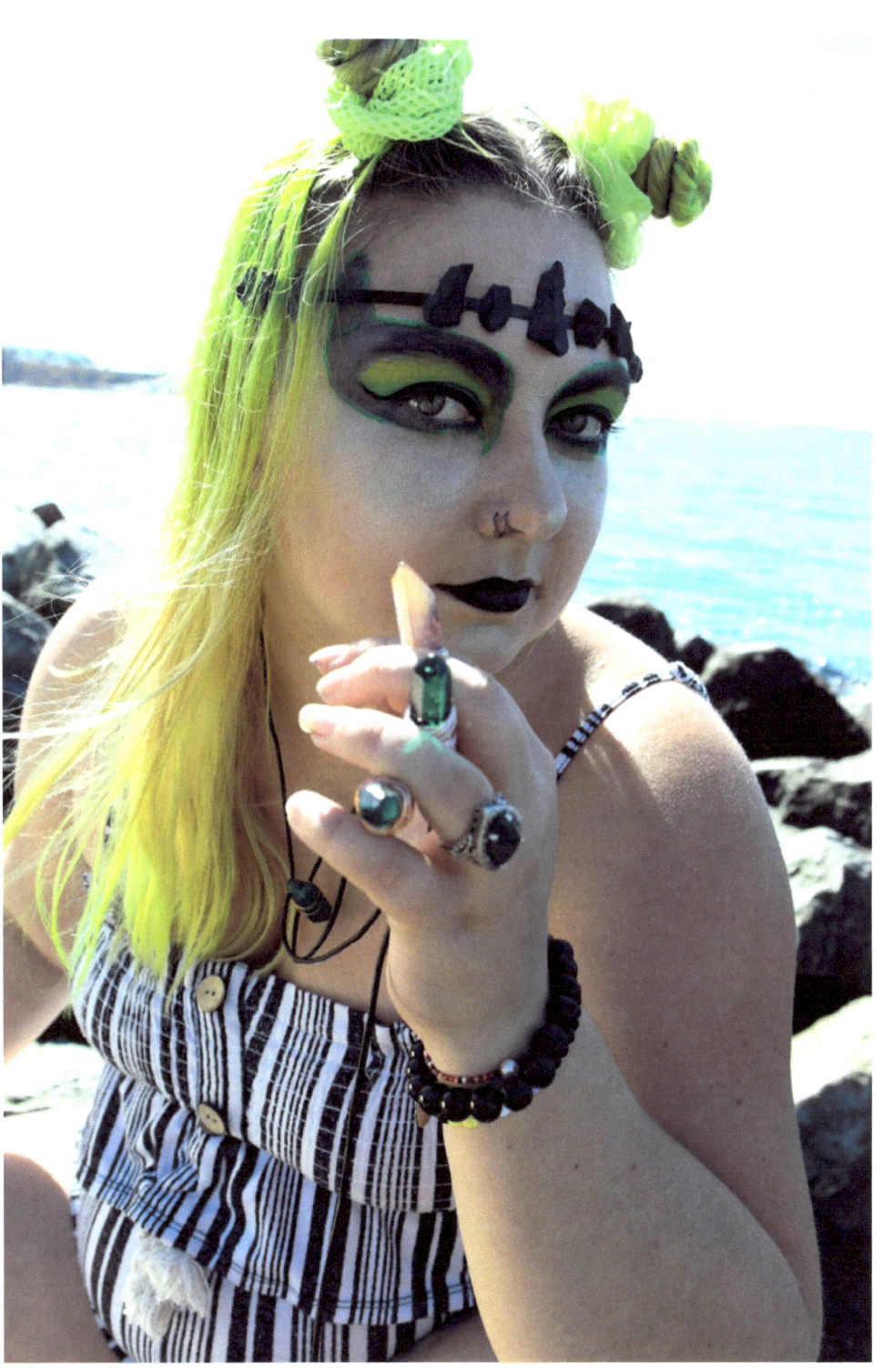

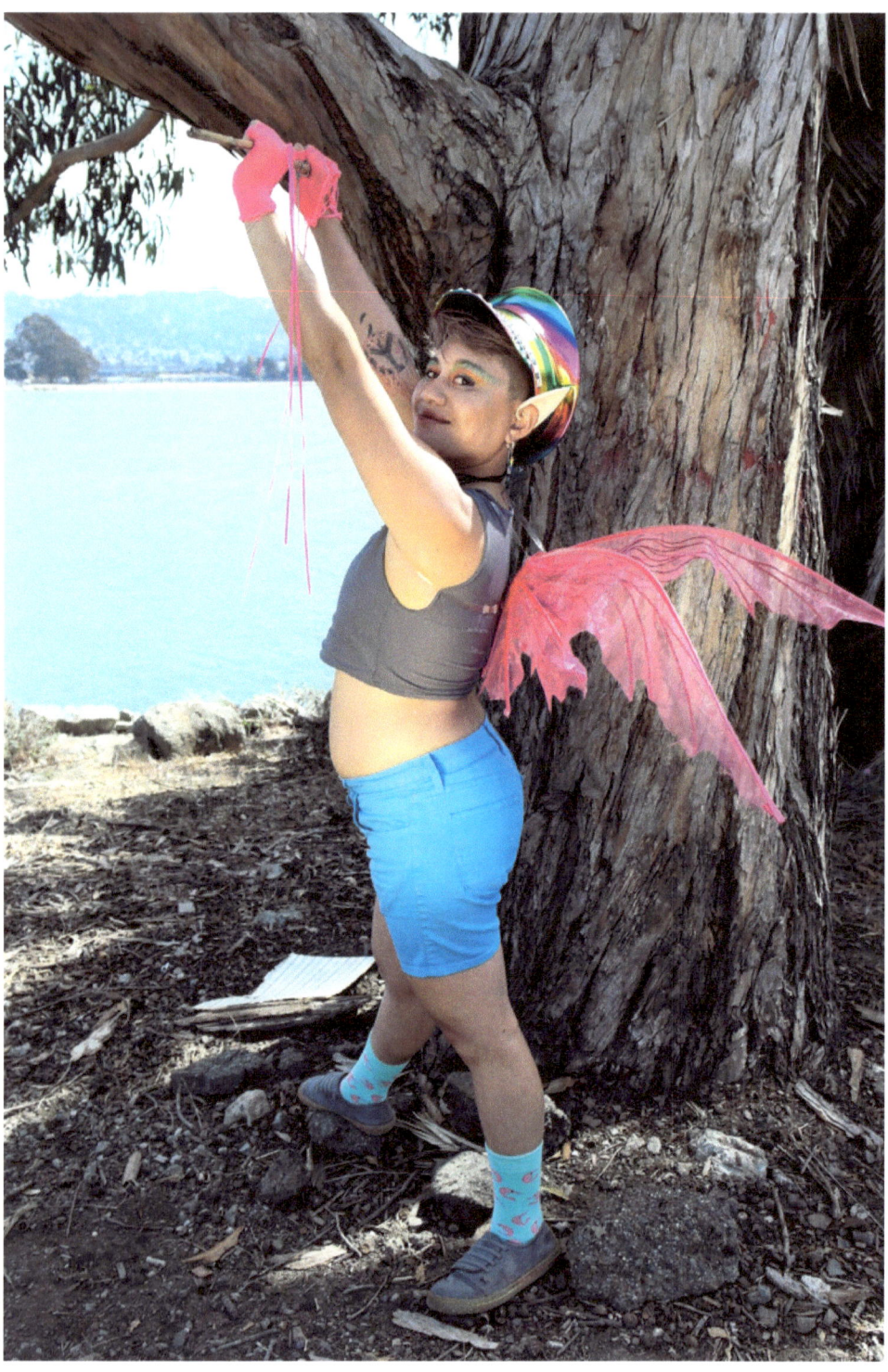

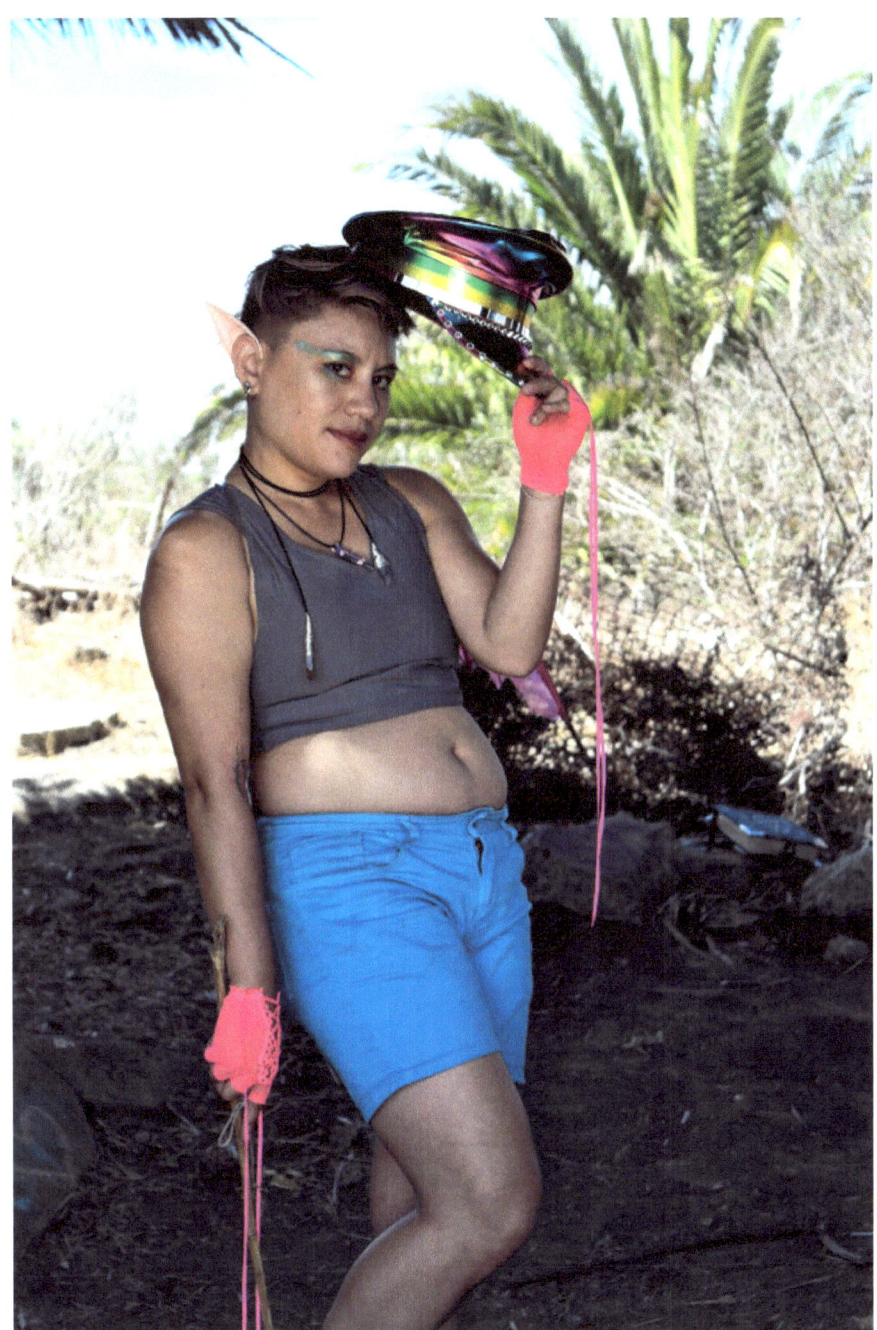

Model: Angel Angeles
Photographer: Marisa Wohlschlaeger
Necklace by Spiritually Stoned Co
Lariat by Gemder Fluid Designs

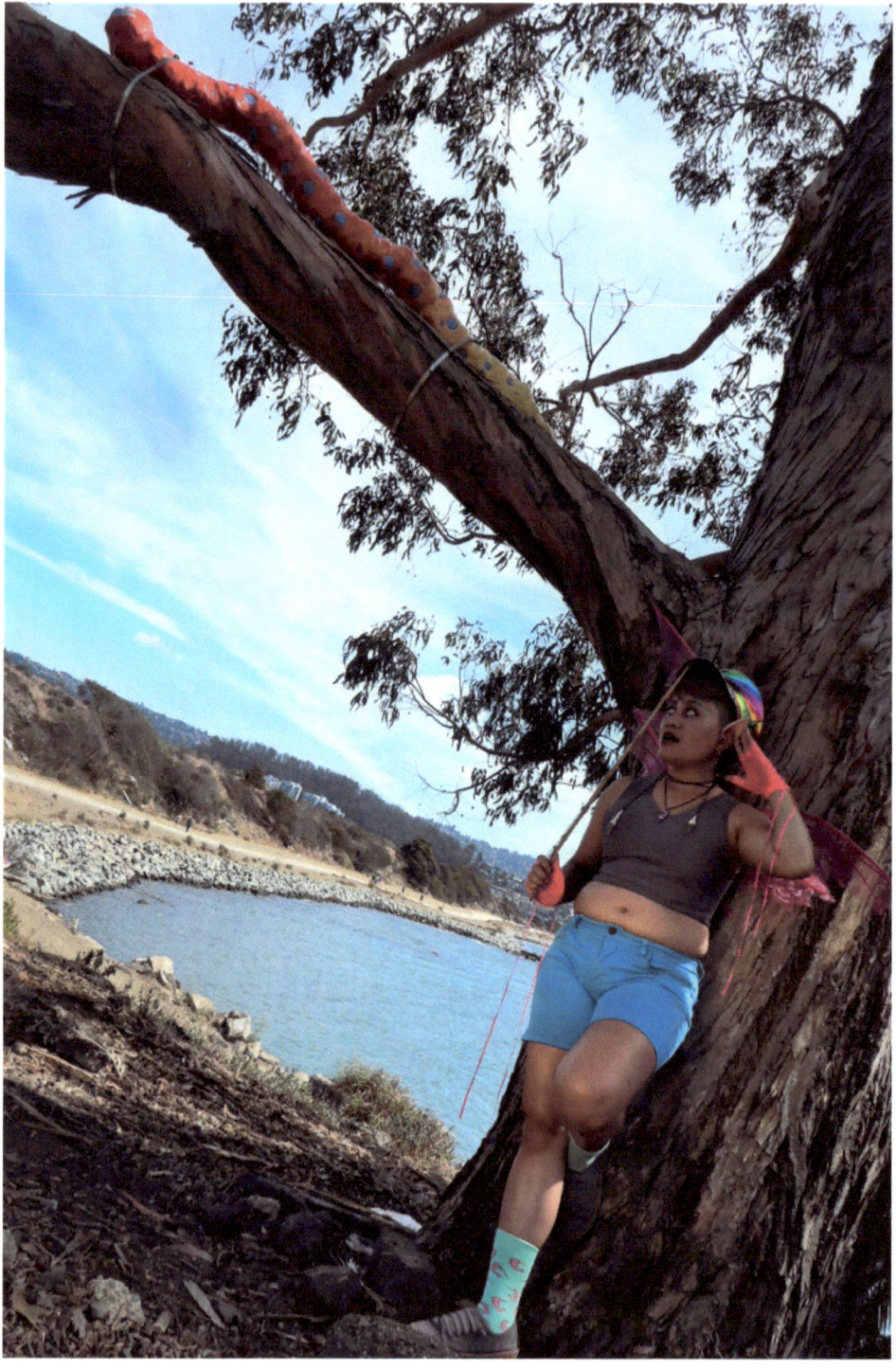

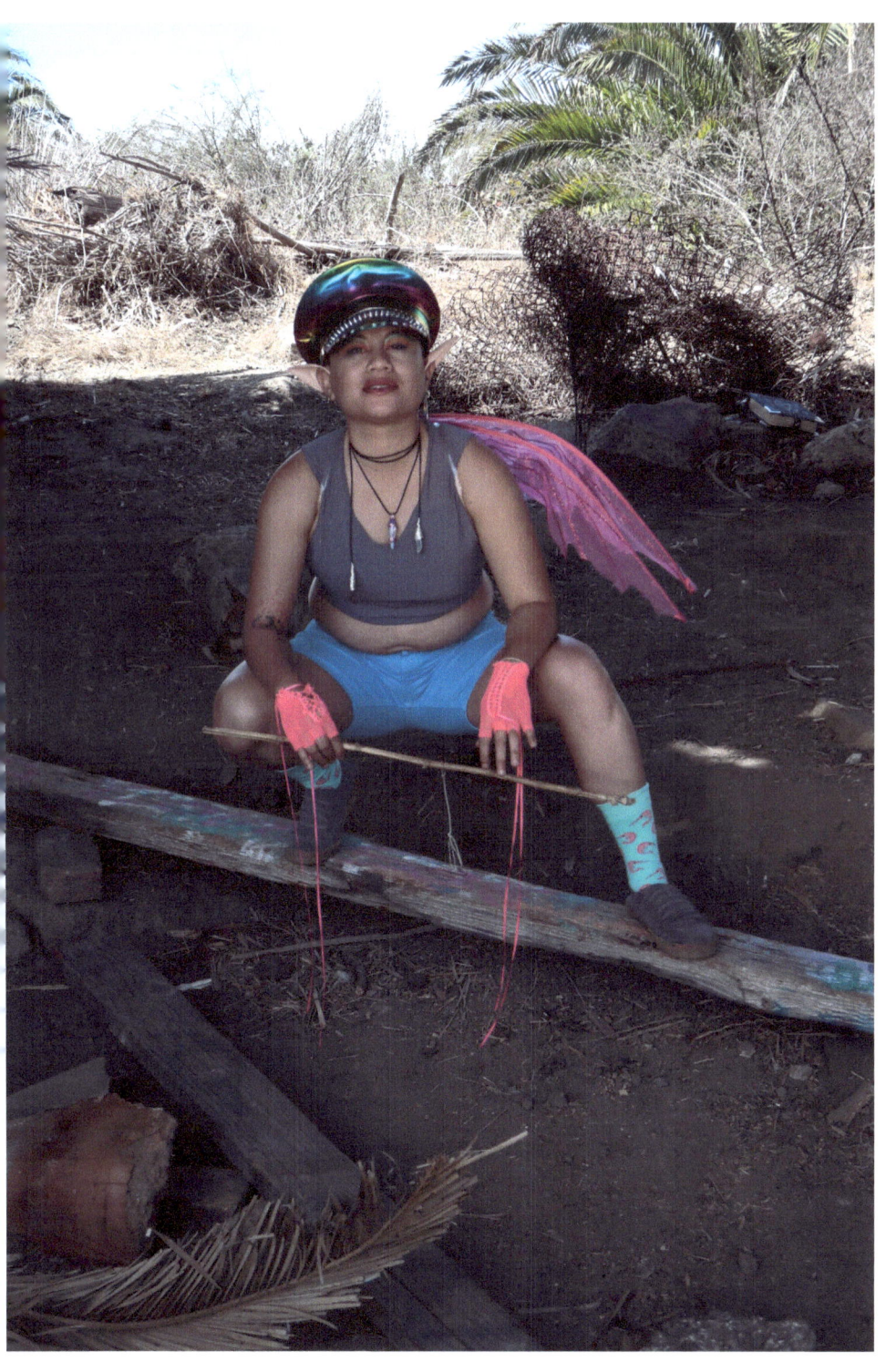

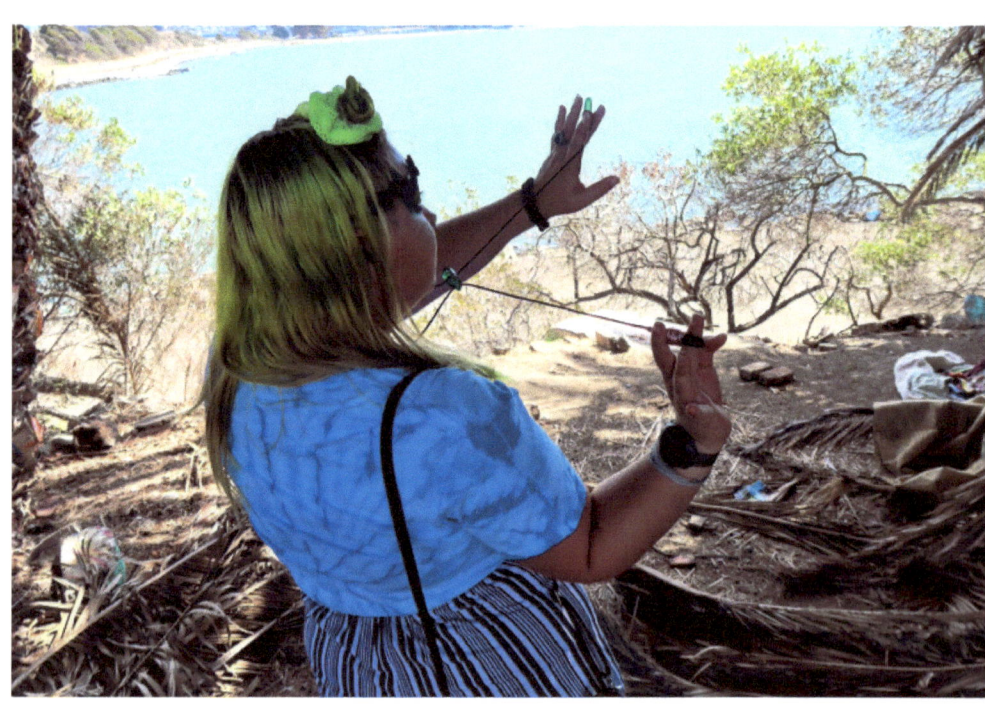

Model: Marisa Wohlschlaeger
Photographer: Angel Angeles
Head jewelry by moniautumn
Lariat by Gemder Fluid Designs
Protect Trans Kids shirt by The Phluid Project

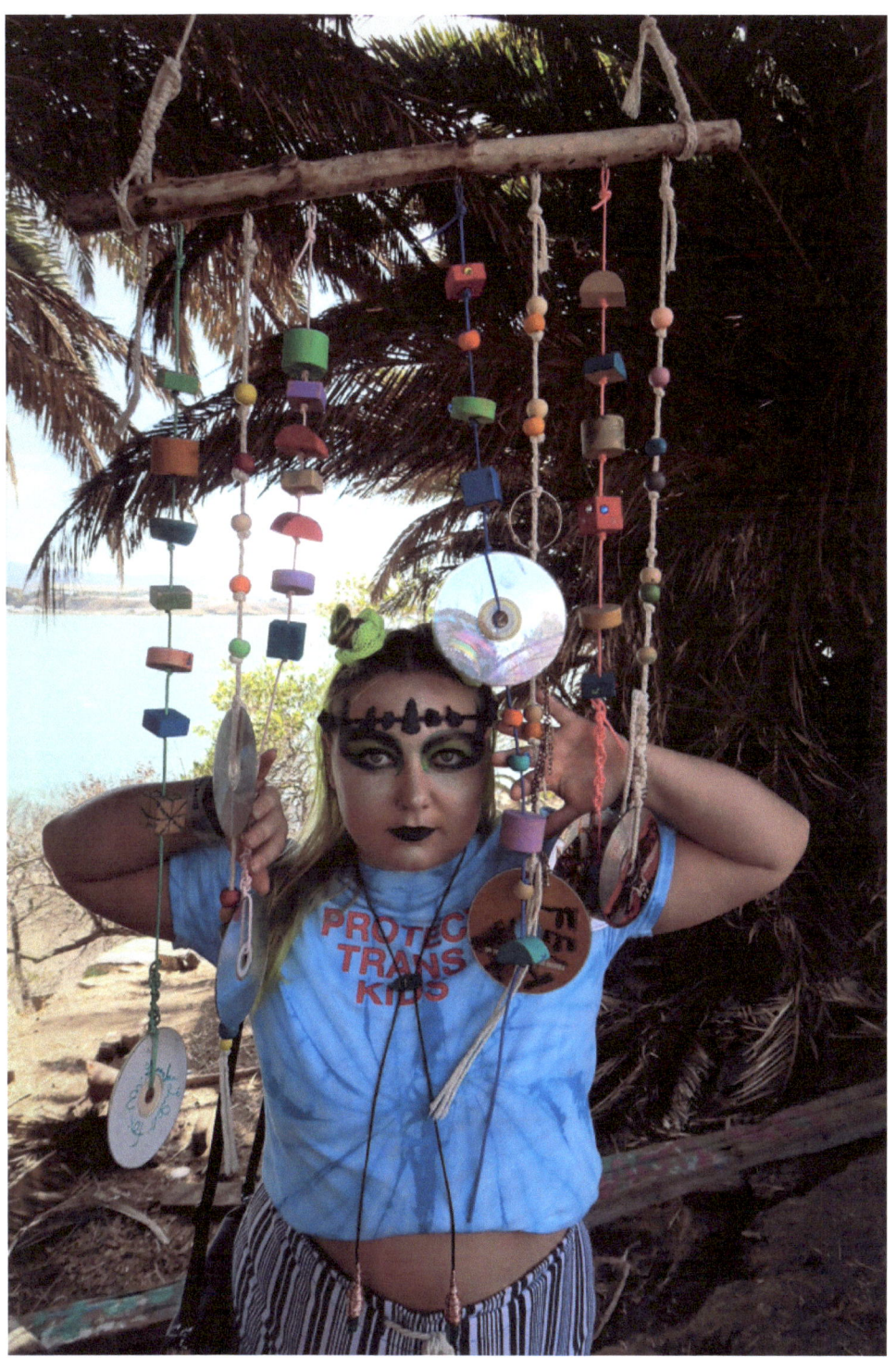

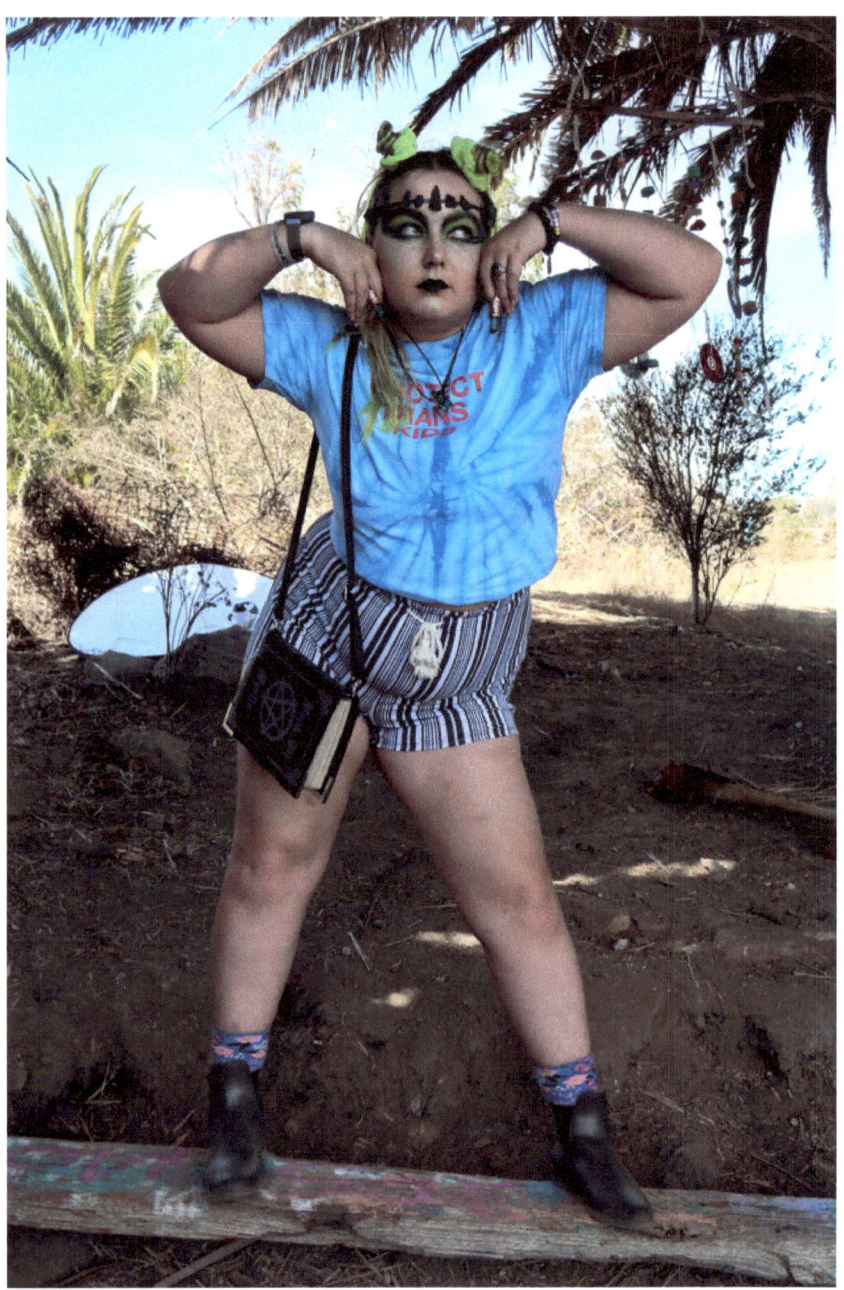

Model: Marisa Wohlschlaeger
Photographer: Angel Angeles
Head jewelry by moniautumn
Lariat by Gemder Fluid Designs
Protect Trans Kids shirt by The Phluid Project

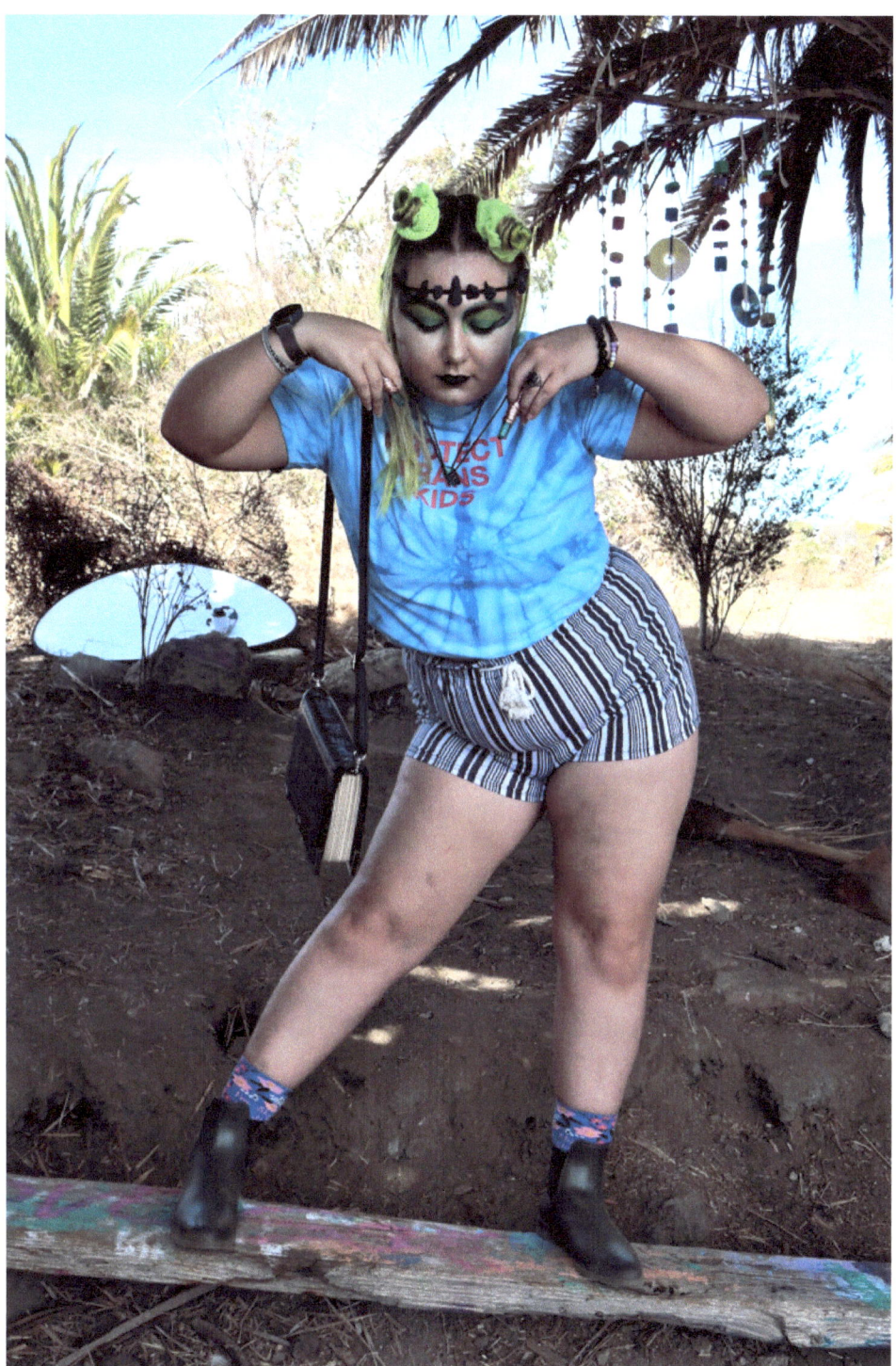

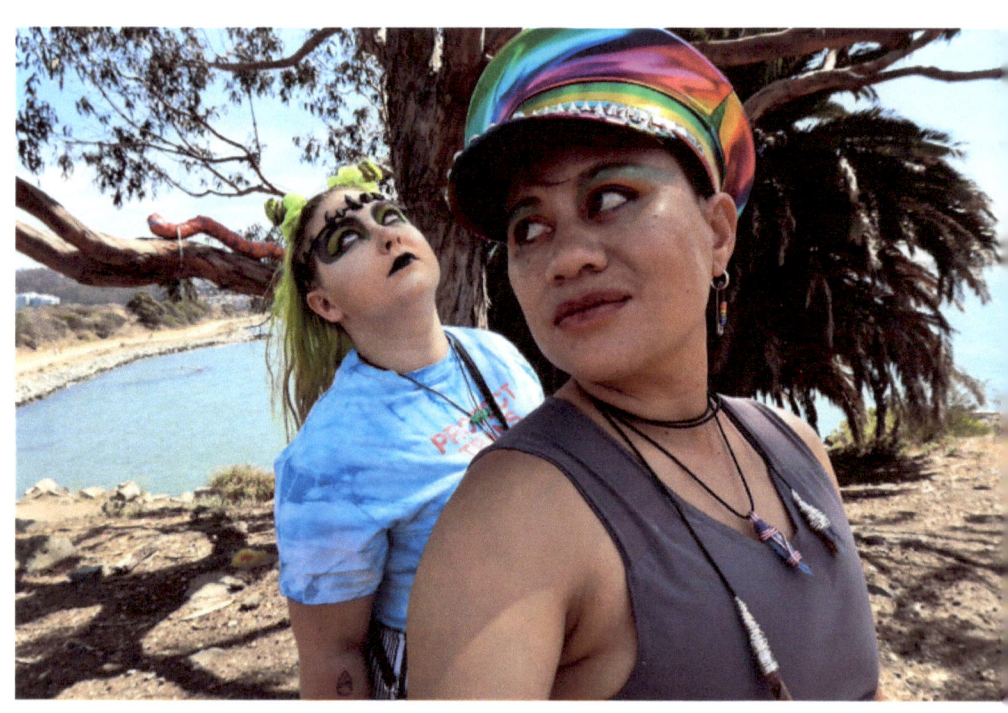

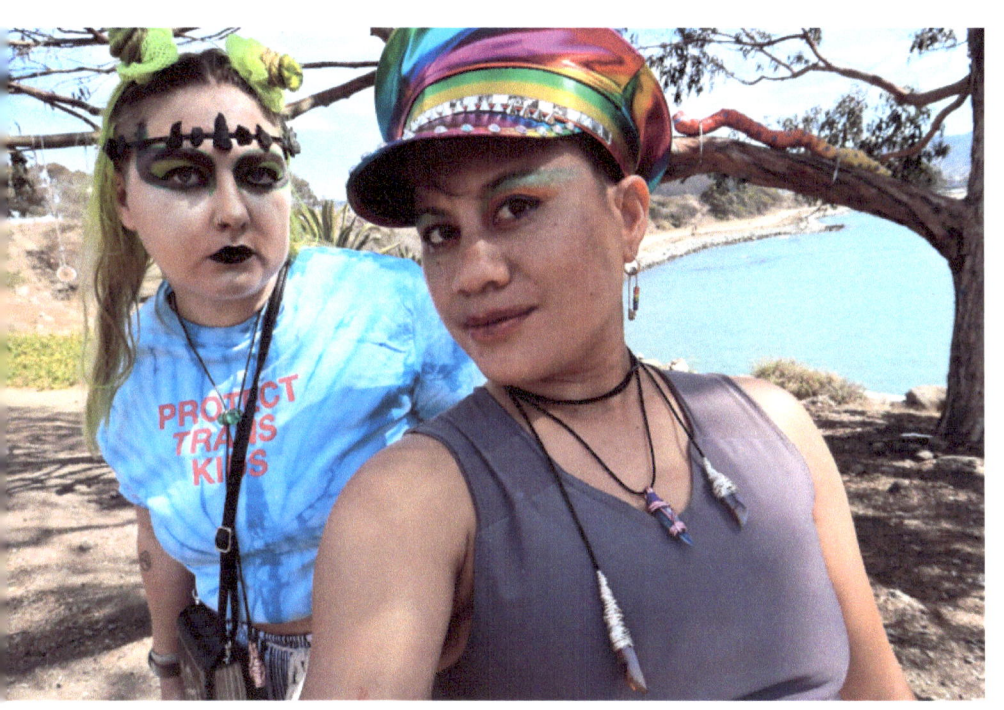

Queer Magic Photo Zine—Albany   October 2021

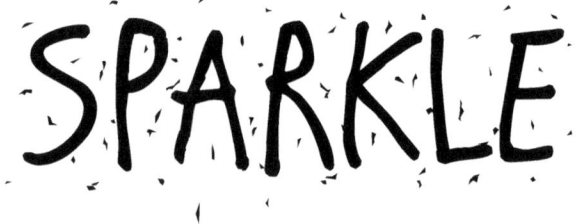

©LOUD & QUEER and Aries I Am Production   Angel Angeles & Marisa Wohlschlaeger

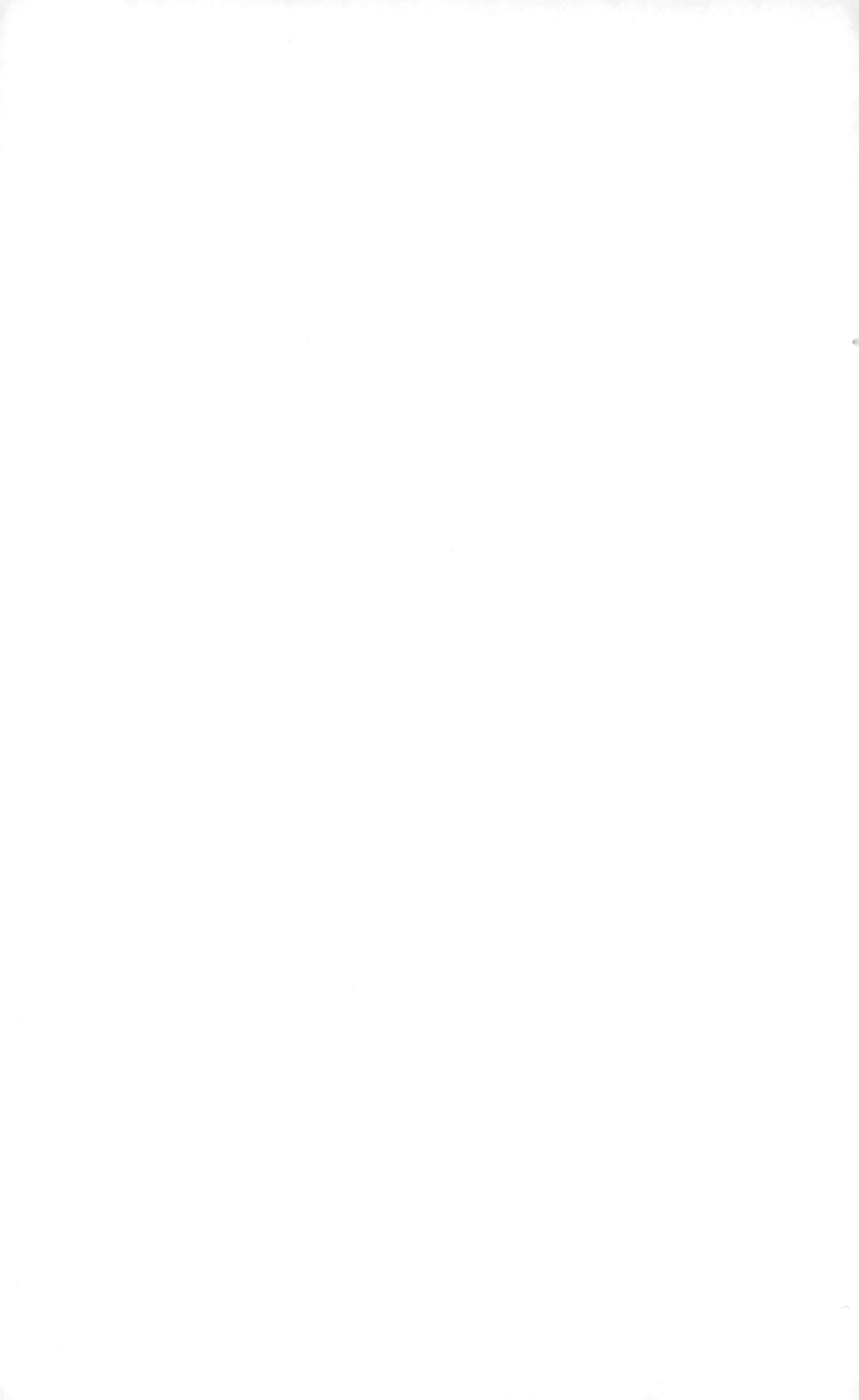

www.ingramcontent.com/pod-product-compliance
Lightning Source LLC
Chambersburg PA
CBHW040331220526
45473CB00009B/2644